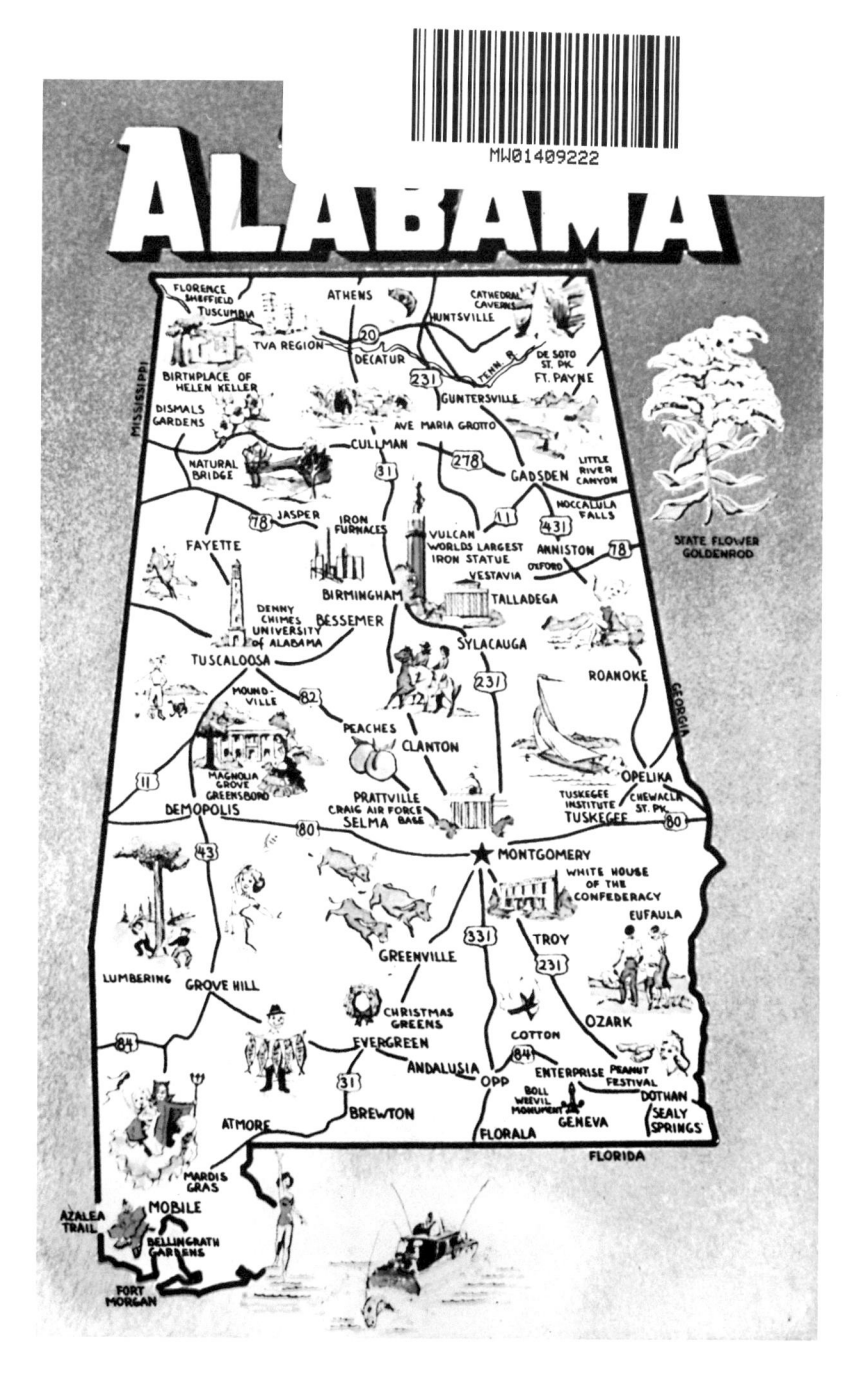

This vintage postcard map of Alabama includes many of the attractions and tourist sites we will be visiting in the pages to come—but naturally, not nearly all of them.

Published by The History Press
Charleston, SC 29403
www.historypress.net

Copyright © 2013 by Tim Hollis
All rights reserved

Cover design by Natasha Walsh

Images are courtesy of the author unless otherwise noted.

First published 2013

Manufactured in the United States

ISBN 978.1.60949.488.9

Library of Congress CIP data applied for.

Notice: The information in this book is true and complete to the best of our knowledge. It is offered without guarantee on the part of the author or The History Press. The author and The History Press disclaim all liability in connection with the use of this book.

All rights reserved. No part of this book may be reproduced or transmitted in any form whatsoever without prior written permission from the publisher except in the case of brief quotations embodied in critical articles and reviews.

See Alabama First

THE STORY OF
ALABAMA TOURISM

TIM HOLLIS

Charleston · London
The History Press

Contents

Introduction. *Everybody Get in the Car* 7

1. Pulling Out of the Driveway 13
2. Stepping on the Accelerator 39

REST STOP 75

3. Putting the Pedal to the Metal 79
4. Slamming on the Brakes 119

REST STOP 147

5. Proceed with Caution 151
6. Heading Toward the Horizon 179

Bibliography 185
About the Author 191

Introduction
Everybody Get in the Car

I would venture a guess that a good number of the people reading these words will already be familiar with at least some of the other books I have done on the subject of tourism history. No, that is not the only thing in my catalogue, but it seems to be a subject that always has still-untapped potential. I have devoted volumes and thousands of words to the history of the attractions in other states, primarily Florida and Tennessee, and now it is time to turn that sort of attention to my home state.

I was born in Birmingham, so it is natural that I have that as my first point of reference. My family didn't travel much for the first few years of my life—my dad being a junior high school teacher and my mom never working outside the home once I was born no doubt had a lot to do with our financial position—but in August 1966, Paw and Maw Hollis managed to scrape up enough dough to send us on our first family vacation, to the Great Smoky Mountains and the wonders of Gatlinburg, Tennessee, and Cherokee, North Carolina.

We must have enjoyed ourselves—or at least some of us did. My mom hated traveling until the day she died. She would much rather have stayed home and watched television with a cat in her lap, but somehow or other, the very next month after our excursion to the Smokies, we were on the road again. This time, we would be sampling more of what Alabama had to offer.

My dad was meticulous in keeping up with postcards and brochures and noting the dates on each of them. From this, I know that we ventured first to Mobile and Dauphin Island on September 9, 1966. Even though I was only

Introduction

Yes, that's the author at age three, touring the decks of the USS *Alabama* in September 1966. The World War II battleship had not been open to tourists for very long at that point.

Introduction

three and a half years old, I do have a few memories of that trip, including an uncomfortable moment at Fort Gaines when some of the prickly cockleburs so common in semi-tropical climates stuck to my socks and felt like a swarm of bees had moved in for the kill. Photos show us prowling the decks of the USS *Alabama*, which had been moved to Mobile and restored as an attraction only the year before. Back on the mainland, we stayed at the small Bamboo Motel in Saraland before continuing the trip to the other side of Mobile Bay and onward to Fort Walton Beach, Florida. The Bamboo Motel might not have been anything spectacular, but I recall reading out the letters on its lighted sign underneath the portico in front of the office. (Yes, I had already learned to read by then.)

During that 1966 trip, somehow my dad must have elected to bypass Alabama's own Gulf Coast in favor of Florida's Miracle Strip, but we made up for that in the summer of 1967 by traveling down to Gulf Shores, Orange Beach and Fort Morgan. By chance, I have a postcard my dad mailed to someone back home from that trip, and to this day, one of his statements is a puzzle to me. After stating that we were having "the time of our lives" (no doubt my mom's attitude about it notwithstanding), my dad wrote that I, especially, was enjoying the water. What is so puzzling about that for a four-year-old, you ask? Simply that no one in my family, including me, ever learned how to swim—so I fail to understand how I could have been enjoying the water except perhaps by just looking at it or dipping my toes into the salty brine. Life's full of unsolved mysteries, isn't it?

From that point onward, we seem to have done a pretty good job of mixing in visits to Alabama's attractions along with our trips to other states. The big difference was that since just about anywhere in Alabama could be reached in only a few hours, except the beaches, we mostly toured the state as short weekend or single-day trips, reserving our longer, more involved drives for other places. Before the 1960s ended, we had visited most of the Alabama attractions at least once. I know that we were back in Mobile again on July 20, 1969, when my dad noted on a postcard that we watched the astronauts land on the moon in our room at a Holiday Inn. (Well, the moon wasn't in our room, but you know what I mean, so lay off the smart remarks.)

Besides saving postcards and brochures, my dad was an avid amateur photographer, so the images he made with his mid-1950s 35mm camera were, in many ways, the record of my life. Only occasionally would there be malfunctions, usually once the camera began getting old. For example, in 1970 we went to Jasmine Hill Gardens to take in the scenery and all the replicas of classic Grecian art, but all of our photos from that visit look

Introduction

like the camera lens was coated with Vaseline. Such anomalies were rare, although I have to admit that once we replaced the old reliable 35mm with Kodak's newer, smaller Pocket Instamatic, the quality of the resulting photos went straight downhill. It is fine and dandy to be nostalgic about the old days, but digital photography is one modern-day improvement that I wish fervently had been available back then.

Just as none of us ever learned to swim, neither were we a camping family, much preferring a carpeted, air-conditioned room in a motel to the great outdoors. (Since our home did not have central air conditioning until 1973, it was indeed a rare treat to spend a hot summer day in the comfort of a Holiday Inn, Best Western or some independent motel.) We would occasionally take a picnic lunch to one of the places frequented by more nature-loving families, such as Sportsman's Lake Park in Cullman or the Guntersville entry in the chain of Yogi Bear's Jellystone Park Campgrounds, but not very often. We visited the now-forgotten Canyon Land Park near Fort Payne in 1974, and my Pocket Instamatic photos of that attraction would have been much better had I managed to keep my finger from in front of the lens in most of them.

So, from an early age I had enough background to do this book but did not really think about how to put it all together until The History Press and I were discussing possible projects to follow the three other books I have done for them. (Counting all of my other publishers too, this is book number twenty-two for me.) No one had ever approached the subject of Alabama's tourism history before, at least not in the way I deal with such subjects, so the project received the green light with a minimum of stress.

I have to single out two employees at Alabama's State Department of Tourism for their enthusiastic support of this book (not completely unselfishly, we imagine). Both Edith Parten and Tommy Cauthen were instrumental in the early stages, with their most invaluable help coming the week of Thanksgiving Day 2011. Cauthen contacted me in a panic, saying that the big boss had ordered that the contents of the department's archival filing cabinets be dumped to make some much-needed room. Cauthen wanted to know how quickly I could make it to Montgomery to pick up the archival materials before they went to the dumpster. I was there the next day, thinking I was going to clean out a couple of four-drawer filing cabinets. Instead, I was confronted with an entire wall of files on every conceivable (and not so conceivable) topic relating to Alabama tourism. I made my way through the file folders, grabbing the ones with labels that seemed to apply to what I was doing, but when my car would not hold anything else, I estimated

INTRODUCTION

Now it's 1974, and future author Tim Hollis is holding up the fence at the nostalgic miniature golf course at Sportsman's Lake Park in Cullman.

that I probably took only about a tenth of what was there. It was the most important tenth, though, and much of the historical information you will read in the following pages was buried deep in those files. So thanks for the advance warning, Edith and Tommy!

That is enough introduction because you did not buy this book to hear my life history. Turn the page and begin learning how Alabama's tourism industry developed slowly at first and then exploded in the 1950s and 1960s before almost imploding by the end of the next decade. However, it rebounded nicely and is now cited as the second-largest industry in the state (trailing the medical profession). Grab your own picnic lunch and come along for the ride—and don't go into the water unless you know how to swim!

Chapter 1
Pulling Out of the Driveway

Alabama's tourism industry, in the true sense of the word, is primarily a product of the 1950s and '60s. The state was definitely a few years behind its neighbors Florida and Tennessee when it came to realizing the full potential of those travelers who happened to be passing through. In fact, prior to World War II, most of Alabama's attractions were intended as much for locals as they were for out-of-state visitors. As we will see in this chapter, the concept of welcoming tourists to Alabama might have been something of a novelty for many years, but every great concept has to begin somewhere. In Alabama's case, the foundation for a future industry was laid primarily in the 1920s and early '30s.

BLOUNT FORCE

In the years immediately following the Civil War, Alabama and most other Southern states were too busy picking up the pieces to think much about tourism, a concept that was almost as foreign as the Yankees who had made their uninvited inroads into the region. When "places to go" did start to become a viable concept, they were largely intended for the wealthier class—and since the automobile was a long way from being invented, they served a railroad clientele.

For those looking for some brief relief from the sweltering Alabama summers, the state's numerous natural springs became logical choices for

5362. The Florida Special Crossing Little Warrior River, near Palos, Alabama.

The first tourists to visit Alabama came by railroad, not by automobile. Even then, most of them were simply passing through on their way to somewhere else, as illustrated by the Florida Special chugging its way through western Jefferson County en route to sun and surf.

cooling off. One of the earliest to be developed for railroad travelers was Blount Springs, where the mineral waters had been a source of pride since the 1830s. In July 1878, the first phase of what would become the landmark Blount Springs Hotel opened, and the community was soon a booming destination, especially for citizens of nearby Birmingham who could ride the rails into the mountains to enjoy its luxuries. As would happen fairly often in the future, it did not take long for Blount Springs to include among those luxuries such entertainment as gambling—via card games, slot machines, roulette wheels and horse racing, all of which were legal at the time.

In 1887, the Blount Springs resort was purchased by brothers J.W. and Mack Sloss, owners of Birmingham's Sloss Furnaces (which would also become a tourist attraction almost a century afterward). The Sloss brothers poured all of their resources into Blount Springs, bringing in such novelties as gas lighting and French chefs from New Orleans to prepare meals for the guests. Their ownership was passed along to successors in the early 1900s, with each new manager promising—and delivering—bigger and better attractions and services. One thing that remained constant, however, was that Blount Springs was strictly a summer resort, boasting a population of nearly three thousand during those months but existing almost as a ghost town the rest of the year.

Times were changing, though, and Blount Springs' role as a showplace of early tourism did not last. The Louisville and Nashville Railroad rerouted in November 1914, and the new tracks bypassed Blount Springs. (This was an eerie foreshadowing of what would happen to many other tourist sites in the 1960s, when their communities were bypassed by the new federal interstate highway program.) The Blount Springs Hotel burned to the ground in June 1915, effectively ending the community's role as a tourist attraction.

The Blount Springs name lives on, of course, and so do the names of many other former resorts from the pre-automobile era. It is said that virtually any Alabama town with "springs" in its name was once, to one degree or another, a tourist attraction. But whether they were ever major destinations or simply local curiosities, each had its part to play in the early years of the tourism industry.

THE SUNNY SOUTH BECKONS

It really should be no surprise that it took so many years for out-of-state tourists to discover Alabama's wide variety of things to see and places to go. In 1900, even Florida was barely out of the crawling stage compared to its later prominence in the tourism industry, and even that was primarily due to the efforts of railroad magnates who were creating seaside resorts for their wealthy cronies to escape the harsh northern winters. Little, if any, thought was given to the rest of the region.

In 1921, author John T. Faris made the most comprehensive survey to date of the oft-overlooked southern states in his book *Seeing the Sunny South*. In the introduction, he acknowledged that most people visiting the South (the implication being that only those from other parts of the country would even be interested) did so by railroad. But then, he felt compelled to deal with the newest emerging form of leisure travel:

> *What a contrast the automobile is! It is so easy-going. You can see up, down and around, and not simply through a narrow window. If the mood takes you, you can go up a side road. You can loiter or you can hurry on. You can see a house, a tree, an orchard, a garden or anything you want. The car is so human.*

Yes, it is good to take the automobile. But it is fine to have the railroad at hand—especially in places where no one has yet seen fit to make a dependable road, or where such a road cannot be made, or where it is absolutely necessary to cover more territory in a given time than can be done with the car.

Ah, yes—the true blockade to touring the South by car was revealed in that second paragraph. Because of the South's primarily rural background, roads had long been low on the to-do list for local and state governments. Shortly, we will examine some of the early efforts to remedy that, but first, back to Faris's book for a moment.

Three entire chapters, and a portion of a fourth, were devoted to Alabama. Naturally, at this stage of the game, there were no "tourist attractions" as such for Faris to highlight; instead, he concentrated mostly on historical sites and elements that would have seemed interesting to those from another part of the country. One chapter dealt totally with Mobile, its history and the varied types of fishing (both saltwater and freshwater) available. In the next chapter, Faris wrote:

It is not easy to realize that Alabama stretches from north to south so far that the two counties bordering on the Gulf of Mexico have nearly three months more of growing weather than the counties to the north of the Tennessee River. But it is not difficult to imagine how eager Alabama is to have more of those counties on the Gulf. Is it to be wondered at that she casts longing eyes on the bit of West Florida that shuts her out from salt water, except for a stretch sixty miles wide?

Inasmuch as there had not been a lot to write about in the future Gulf Shores environs, Faris then moved his discussion to inland historic towns, including Demopolis, Greensboro and Tuscaloosa, taking a couple of sentences to acknowledge the mounds in the northern part of Hale County: "The scientist has departed, but the grass-grown mounds still give a welcome to the traveler who rests in their shade." Alabama would be making more than a molehill out of those mounds during the next decade.

Faris's tour continued with Russellville, Tuscumbia, Sheffield and Florence, moving east to Huntsville and Guntersville:

Within easy reach of Guntersville are mountains, not lofty, perhaps, but always attractive. Lookout Mountain, at whose foot nestles Gadsden on the Coosa, another of the state's bustling steel cities, is notable, among other reasons, because of beautiful Noccalula Falls, where the water drops 96 feet.

Then Faris moved along to Anniston, Talladega (where there were no NASCAR racers nor a track for them to race on), Tallassee and, finally, an extended discussion of Montgomery and its role in Confederate history.

It is somewhat notable that Faris chose to devote an entire chapter to the topic "In the Shadow of Birmingham's Red Mountain," in that Birmingham had existed for only fifty years at the time of his book. Therefore, rather than focusing on history (most of which was still the future for the city), Faris expounded on the mighty steel mills that gave Birmingham its reputation. He mentions only one named road: the Montgomery Highway, described as visible from the crest of Red Mountain as it worked its way south. It would soon be joined on Alabama maps by some even more highly promoted brethren of the highway fraternity.

The Senator's Road

In his excellent book *Dirt Roads to Dixie* (1991), Howard Lawrence Preston devotes much space to describing the beginnings of what would become known as the "good roads movement" in the early years of the twentieth century. Space does not permit as thorough a discussion here, but as the story relates to Alabama, one tenet remained true. There was a constant struggle for funds between those who wanted the nation's highways improved so as to better serve tourists (and, ergo, the business owners who existed to serve them) and those whose primary concern was the farmer and his needs for getting his goods to nearby markets. Money and power usually having the most clout, the former group won out, and there was a concerted effort to develop clearly labeled highways to get automobile travelers from Point A to Point B with a minimum of aggravation.

The first transcontinental route, the Lincoln Highway, was assembled piece by piece and completed by 1913. Almost immediately thereafter, another movement was begun to establish a similar transcontinental route through the southern half of the country. The Lincoln Highway had a legendary reputation, but it did traverse a part of the country where the going might not be so good during the winter months. A route was proposed that would

Senator John Hollis Bankhead was an early proponent for better highways, and in tribute to him, a major roadway connecting Washington, D.C., with San Diego, California, was named for him. Two-lane stretches of road across the country, including in Alabama, still bear that designation.

link Washington, D.C., with San Diego, California, and the politico in the first of those two cities who sponsored the legislation was John Hollis Bankhead of Alabama. As a member of the House of Representatives, and later as a senator, Bankhead was well known for his support of the Good Roads Program, and with his considerable political influence, the route was finally approved. Since Bankhead's hometown was Jasper, it did not take a media pundit (had there been one in those days) to know that he would arrange to have this new coast-to-coast highway pass through Alabama and, specifically, through his town.

As it turned out, Bankhead died in 1920, just before the process of tying up all the loose ends was finished, and in his honor the new automobile trail was christened the Bankhead Highway. It entered Alabama just east of Heflin, proceeded to Birmingham, turned northwest to Jasper and exited the state en route to Tupelo, Mississippi, before continuing its long western trek to the Pacific Ocean. As with most such early federal highways, the Bankhead was put together by a combination of existing roads and new construction, and several pieces of that old, original alignment can still be found in the back streets of various towns along its route.

By the time the Bankhead Highway received its official name in 1921, other federal highways were being developed, but few with the Atlantic-to-Pacific scope of that one. The Old Spanish Trail traversed the Florida Panhandle, connecting St. Augustine with Southern California, but its route across Alabama, near Mobile, was a short one. The Lee Highway ran from New York City to New Orleans, coming into Alabama at the northeastern corner, passing through Birmingham and Tuscaloosa and then entering Mississippi. The Andrew Jackson Highway connected Chicago and New Orleans, running through the middle of Alabama and down to Mobile Bay. All of these routes, sometimes under other names, became Alabama's major tourist corridors in the coming years.

Bottleneck at Auburn

Sometimes highways received local names that were not officially part of the federal government's fledgling program. The aforementioned Montgomery Highway through Birmingham was one of these (it was technically a part of the Andrew Jackson Highway), and another was the stretch from Birmingham to Auburn, which became known as the Florida Short Route because it was the most efficient way of getting to the Sunshine State's Atlantic coast. At that time, there was nothing to see in the Panhandle, so future resorts such as Panama City Beach were not part of the equation.

By 1924, there were enough travelers that a new breed of business had been born: the roadside attraction. One of Alabama's first was found along that same Florida Short Route, approximately five miles north of Auburn. It was known simply as "the Bottle," and for good reason. It was a sixty-four-foot-tall wooden replica of a bottle of orange Nehi soda, constructed by John F. Williams of Opelika, who just happened to own the Nehi bottling plant for that town. The Bottle contained a grocery store and service station on its ground floor, with a spiral staircase inside that led to the upper portions. From windows in the Bottle's neck, tourists could view the surrounding countryside.

For a lamentably short time in the 1920s, the Bottle was a sight to see along the future U.S. 280 as it approached Opelika and Auburn. The giant orange soft drink bottle featured an observation deck atop its cap.

    Although the Bottle did its job admirably, becoming a landmark on the Florida Short Route, its career was brief. As with most such wooden structures of the day, fire was a constant worry, and sure enough, the Bottle burned to the ground in 1933. It was probably the Depression that prevented it from being rebuilt, but it was never totally forgotten. Even on today's maps of U.S. 280 (still designated as the Florida Short Route), there is a dot marking its location as simply "The Bottle, Alabama." But not to worry—it would hardly be the final roadside attraction to exist to give road-weary tourists a place to stop and possibly separate them from a few of their dollars in the bargain.

The Highway Numbers Game

About the same time the Bottle was raising its big orange drink over the plains of southeastern Alabama, there was some further talk in Washington about the nation's federal highways. The idea of named routes (Lee Highway, Bankhead Highway and so on) seemed to be a great one, except that with an increase of traffic on them, their signage and alignment was getting to be rather confusing. Each highway was marked by its designated colored emblem painted on posts and markers, and since routes frequently overlapped, it took a very skilled (and sharp-eyed) driver to be able to follow them. The highway department decided to scrap the names and begin assigning numbers to U.S. roads, which would be clearly marked by black numbers and letters against a white background shaped like a shield.

By 1926, numbers were replacing names throughout the country, including in Alabama. The process of numbering the highways was not done by some willy-nilly, pull-a-number-out-of-a-hat method. The first decision was that highways running north–south would have odd numbers, and east–west highways would bear even numbers. The most important highways bore single-digit numbers, as

Prior to 1925, federal U.S. highways had names rather than numbers. The Andrew Jackson Highway followed what would largely become the route of U.S. 31. This postcard was mailed from Huntsville in August 1927, while names were slowly giving way to their more famous designations.

JUNCTION U. S. HIGHWAY NO. 29 NEW YORK - NEW ORLEANS

Generally speaking, the intersection of any two major tourist highways would be a catalyst for immense commercial development. This neighborhood in Opelika seems to have avoided that for the present, but the card still proudly points out the junction of U.S. 29 (New York to New Orleans) and U.S. 241 (Chicago to Miami).

with U.S. 1, which ran from the Canada border with Maine to Key West, Florida. But it did not stop there. The major east–west transcontinental highways were given even numbers (20, 30, 40 and so on), progressing from north to south. (When the federal interstate highway program was introduced in the 1950s, the same rules applied, but in order to not cause confusion, the numbers went in reverse order, with I-10 running along the Gulf Coast and higher numbers as one moved north.) There were also three-digit numbers for highways that were considered "branches" of the main routes.

In Alabama, the former Bankhead Highway largely became U.S. 78. The Lee Highway became U.S. 11 and the Andrew Jackson Highway was U.S. 31. The former Old Spanish Trail was U.S. 90. Most of these had their own "branches," such as U.S. 31's relatives U.S. 231, U.S. 331 and U.S. 431. Although portions of each of these can still be found with their former names—usually along stretches that had been bypassed by wider and straighter routes—these were the highway numbers with which most modern-day travelers are familiar, and they will be turning up over and over again as we progress through the pages that follow.

Parks for Everyone

Most people were probably still trying to get their heads around the idea of a long family vacation when the State of Alabama took a giant step toward establishing what would become some of its most popular non-commercialized attractions. In 1927, the state legislature passed the State Land Act, which paved the way for Alabama's first state parks.

Randy Jinks of the Alabama State Parks Department kindly provided an unpublished manuscript about the establishment of that string of future attractions. Most of it deals with activity since the 1960s, but as far as the early years, we can learn:

> *The first Alabama State Park, an area of 421 acres, was established in Talladega County in 1930. Early records show this as Talladega County State Park, but no further information is available as to development or final disposition of the area.*
>
> *By 1933, the state of Alabama had acquired eleven state parks, comprising a total of 6,075 acres. However, only two of these areas, Cheaha and Little River (now Claude Kelley), evolved into today's State Parks System.*

Indeed, according to the department's chronological list showing when each state park was acquired, nearly half were already established before World War II. Besides the two 1933 entries mentioned above, the others that came about during and immediately after the Great Depression were Paul M. Grist (1934); Chattahoochee, Chewacla, Chickasaw, DeSoto, Gulf, Monte Sano and Oak Mountain (all in 1935); and Bladon Springs (1936). It may seem a bit strange that such a bleak economic period in United States history could have produced so many attractions that are still being enjoyed today (Alabama was particularly hard hit by the Depression, especially the steelmaking plants), but that period of financial woe produced one concept that went a long, long way toward getting the parks off the ground—or out of the woods, whichever you prefer.

The Civilian Conservation Corps (CCC), which worked closely with the National Park Service, was dispatched to Alabama to aid in the improvement of the state parks. As Randy Jinks's history explains:

> *The developments installed under the CCC included roads, cabins, lodges, cottages, picnic shelters, hiking trails, swimming areas with bath houses,*

SEE ALABAMA FIRST

4—Bunker Tower, at Cheaha State Park between Talladega and Anniston, Ala.

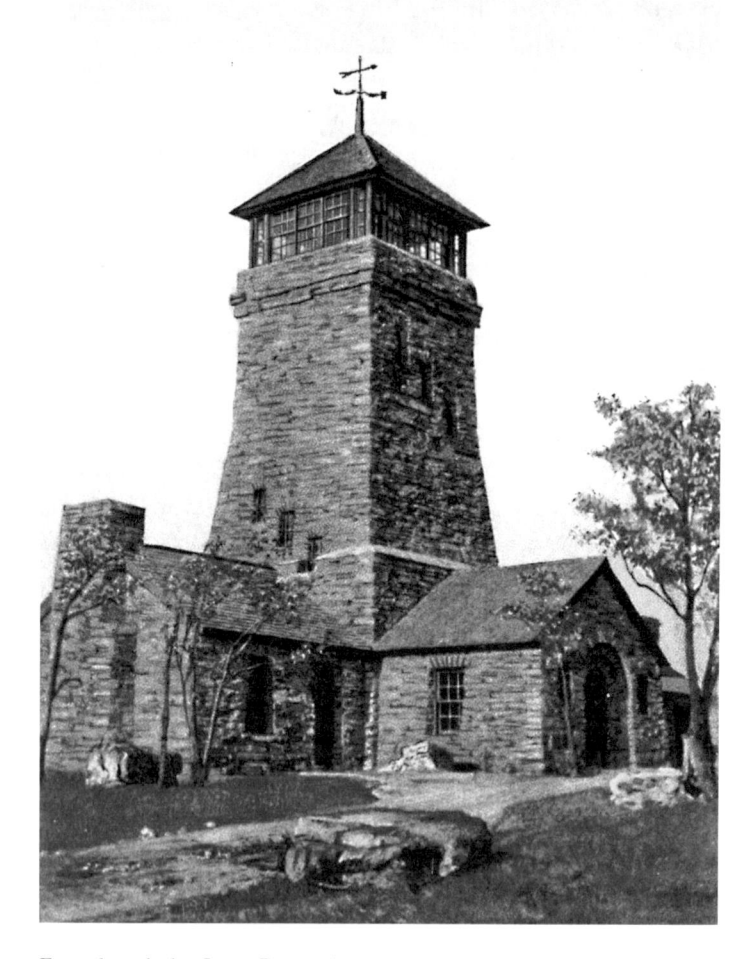

Even though the Great Depression put a damper on tourism development, the work of government-directed groups such as the WPA and CCC was instrumental in developing Alabama's fledgling state parks program. This observation tower at Cheaha State Park is still one of the most visited spots in that whole system.

lakes, beaches and other recreational facilities. These park areas and the facilities developed under the CCC program formed the nucleus of the present-day parks system.

Even today, it is easy to recognize the work the CCC did at these parks because it was almost as distinctive as having its own trademark. Virtually everything built by the CCC was surfaced with native stone, from the tourist cabins to the huge observation tower atop Mount Cheaha, the highest point in the state. While some CCC structures were allowed to fall into disrepair over the years—and are the occasional targets of renovation today—the ones that remain are unmistakable and a valuable link to the beginning of Alabama's interest in tourism.

This got even better in 1939, with the official establishment of the State Parks Division. The new department chose five of the parks in which the CCC had done the most work as candidates for more extensive improvement. Those five were Cheaha, Chewacla, DeSoto, Gulf and Monte Sano. A concerted effort was made to get these five parks ready for the spring of 1939 by increasing the amount of housekeeping equipment in their cabins. The history reports that cabin rental rates during the 1939 season ranged from $1.25 to $3.00 per night (the latter being for a crowd of four people), and that by the end of September, the state's total revenue from the parks was a bit over $9,500.

We might be getting slightly ahead of ourselves here, but before temporarily leaving the state parks discussion, it is probably just as well to go ahead and point out that the U.S. involvement in World War II beginning in late 1941 almost spelled doom for the whole program. With virtually every able-bodied male serving in the military, there was a definite shortage of workers to maintain the facilities. In some cases, the parks were closed to the public because of the lack of upkeep. Never fear, though, as things would get brighter in the postwar years. That story will have to wait until our next chapter.

GARDENS OF EDEN

While the state was getting its program of official parks underway, over in the private sector there was also some movement toward what would become some of Alabama's most highly prized (and promoted) tourist attractions.

For one of the earliest, we need to take a trip approximately twenty miles south of Mobile.

Walter D. Bellingrath was ten years old when his family moved from their native Atlanta to Alabama in 1879, and in 1903 he moved to what would prove to be his permanent home city, Mobile. He became a successful Coca-Cola bottler for that city, and he soon married local girl Bessie Morse. In 1917, the Coca-Cola couple found a piece of property they intended to use as a fishing lodge, and one look at its beauty convinced them it was the real thing.

It seems Bessie had quite an affinity for the azaleas that made springtime in the southland a colorful riot each year, so she began planting azalea bushes in the woods surrounding her husband's would-be fishing lodge. The idea grew as rapidly as the azaleas; the couple's biography explains what happened next:

> *In 1927, on a trip to Europe, the Bellingraths were enormously impressed by the great gardens they found there. They decided to call upon professional landscape architects to help them in their labor of love on the Isle-aux-Oies River. The aid of George B. Rogers, internationally known landscape designer and architect, was enlisted and the major aspects of the transformation were begun.*

It is not recorded at just what point the Bellingraths moved from the idea of a private lodge to a park that would bring in people from across the state, the region, the nation and the world. It happened relatively quickly, though, because opening day for the new Bellingrath Gardens was announced as May 3, 1932; they obviously did a good job getting the word out because the story has been told ever since how traffic became hopelessly snarled on the road leading to the gardens, prompting police assistance to untangle the mess. That convinced the couple to begin charging a nominal admission fee to enjoy their handiwork, simply as a way to cut down on the traffic congestion.

Almost from the beginning, Bellingrath Gardens promoted itself as the "charm spot of the Deep South," and few would have disagreed. The couple was so pleased with the location that in 1935 they had their favorite architect George Rogers design a new home for them, situated in the gardens. Neither Bessie Bellingrath nor Rogers got to enjoy it for very long, though, as she died in 1943, and architect Rogers passed away in 1945. Walter Bellingrath continued living in the home until his own death at age eighty-six in 1955.

While the photographs taken in the gardens from 1932 until the present day tend to look much the same, there is one sure line of demarcation between the two principal eras in the attraction's history. Prior to Bellingrath's death, the brochures and advertisements refer only to Bellingrath Gardens. After 1955, the name became "Bellingrath Gardens and Home" because part of Walter's wish was that his own house be opened to the public once he was no longer living. Since then, visitors have been able to marvel at the garden plantings outdoors and the incredible collection of antiques and rare art objects the Bellingraths used to decorate the interior of their home.

At almost exactly the same time the Bellingraths began transforming swampland into a showplace, up in Wetumpka another successful businessman and his wife had almost exactly the same idea. Benjamin Fitzpatrick and his wife, Mary, had made their fortune by founding a southern chain of mercantile establishments known as the L.F.M. Stores (the initials representing the three partners, Leonard-Fitzpatrick-Mueller). By 1927, Fitzpatrick had sold his interest in the company, and he and his wife were free to spend their accumulated money any way they pleased.

What pleased them was the art and architecture of ancient Greece, and they set out to surround their 1830s-era house with a garden devoted to that

Bellingrath Gardens opened just south of Mobile in 1932 and became famous for its lush plantings and the magnificent Walter Bellingrath home.

subject. In fact, as the official history puts it, "the Fitzpatricks made over twenty trips to Greece to purchase their art objects, to study at the American Classical School in Athens, and to simply enjoy Greek culture." Back home, their new development became known as Jasmine Hill Gardens, with the grounds dotted with replicas of classic Grecian sculptures.

Unlike Bellingrath Gardens, Jasmine Hill Gardens was more of a private hobby that just happened to attract more and more tourists as the years went on, but the Fitzpatricks were happy to show off the fruits of their many years of work. In 1971, they turned over control of Jasmine Hill Gardens to Jim and Elmer Inscoe, who have carried on the tradition.

Mounds of History

You may recall that when James T. Faris was listing the historical sights to be seen in Alabama back in 1921, he mentioned the proliferation of Native American mounds in the northern part of Hale County. He stated that the archaeologists had already come and gone by that time, and that was true at the point he was writing his book. However, it was not many years afterward that things began to get active around the site again.

Most of the publicity referred to the mysterious piles of earth as "prehistoric Indian mounds," but they were not prehistoric in the same way as, say, the mythological world of the Flintstones. This civilization thrived from approximately AD 1200 to 1500, making them prehistoric only so far as the known history of North America is concerned. Be that as it may, in the centuries afterward, a settlement called Carthage was established nearby, and in 1897, Carthage changed its name to Moundville. The archeological expeditions Faris mentioned took place primarily in 1905–06, conducted by the Philadelphia Academy of Natural Sciences.

After the Moundville Historical Society was formed in 1923, and the Alabama Museum of Natural History purchased 175 acres near Moundville—which included most of the mounds—in 1928, things could get back to business. In 1933, while Alabama was trying to establish its first state parks, Mound State Park was one of these, but as we saw a few pages back, it is acknowledged as not being one that evolved into a present-day state park. Instead, in 1938 it was renamed Mound State Monument and grew to include 301 acres straddling the Hale/Tuscaloosa County line, taking in all of the mounds that could be identified.

T-27—Indian Mound, showing Part of Burial Ground, near Tuscaloosa, Alabama

At Moundville, the museum originally displayed dozens of Native American skeletons, left just as they were discovered when the earth around them was excavated. Today, the bones are respectfully hidden from public viewing.

WE VISITED MOUND STATE MONUMENT MOUNDVILLE, ALABAMA

No matter how lofty its ideals, almost any tourist attraction of the 1940s or 1950s would supply bumper stickers, and Mound State Monument was in there sticking bumpers with the best of them.

Just as the CCC had helped with the improvements at the state parks, so too did the Depression-era employer go to work at Mound State Monument, among other things completing the centerpiece, the Archeological Museum, in 1939. The physical design of this museum building was patterned after the motifs used by the Native Americans on their pottery and other artifacts that had been discovered on the property and would be displayed within it; however, that was not its most unusual feature.

The site chosen for the building sat directly between two burial grounds, which according to the archaeologists meant the inhabitants of the village usually buried their departed members underneath the dirt floors of their own houses. The skeletons that were unearthed were left in exactly the spot and position in which they were found, with two wings of the museum constructed over and around them. This meant the north wing of the museum contained seventeen former Moundville citizens and the south wing displayed an additional forty. In between the two cadaver collections, the main hall contained the many relics that had been dug up, plus dioramas illustrating how the village would have looked when the denizens were alive and moving rather than lying prone in the two wings. In case anyone has to be told, this sort of exhibition is frowned upon today, but for more than thirty years, it gave visitors to Mound State Monument a chance to get more up close and personal with Moundville's original population than they ever would again.

Cullman's Hail Mary Pass

As we have already seen, and will see again, some tourist attractions were originally conceived to be just that, while others gained that reputation purely by accident. The next of Alabama's big tourism draws to open in the 1930s fell firmly into the latter category, and its founder was about as far from being a tourism tycoon as could be imagined.

Joseph Zoettl was born in Bavaria in 1878, but in 1892 he moved to Alabama to begin his studies at the new St. Bernard Abbey in Cullman. His original intent was to become a priest, but while hoisting a bell into the abbey tower, he wrenched his back permanently out of shape and effectively ended that ambition. Instead becoming a brother in the Benedictine Order, he went to work in the abbey's power plant in 1910 and decided to find a way to occupy his surplus spare time.

The Story of Alabama Tourism

Joseph Zoettl, a Benedictine monk, was crippled by a back injury during his youth, but he spent the rest of his life turning concrete and discarded doodads into the replicas that populated "Little Jerusalem" and the Ave Maria Grotto at St. Bernard's Abbey in Cullman.

This is the central structure of Ave Maria Grotto, the eponymous grotto itself. The idea of a monument of this scope being constructed single-handedly by a stooped Benedictine monk has proved inspirational to visitors of all religious faiths.

Although religious studies were the order of the order, one of the priests raised necessary funds for the college by running a souvenir shop in the main building. Seeing that Brother Joseph, as everyone knew him, enjoyed working with cement and concrete, the priest asked his colleague to fashion some miniature religious shrines to sell. They turned out so well, and their sale raised so much money for the college, that Brother Joseph soon found himself spending more and more of his time elbow deep in cement.

He determined that he would create a "Little Jerusalem," depicting all the holy sites of that city via his miniatures. When he set up the display on the monastery's recreation grounds, so many visitors came to see it that the abbot became alarmed that the college's sacred mission was about to be compromised. A new location in an abandoned rock quarry was decided on, and as the centerpiece, Brother Joseph went to work on his biggest and most spectacular creation: the Ave Maria Grotto. There could be no better description of this awesome sight than the one given in the attraction's 1965 souvenir booklet:

> *This creation is a cave, roofed and covered with artificial stalactites, containing an altar of Alabama marble, mosaicked to perfection with small pieces of limestone and Florida seashells. Above the altar are statues of the Blessed Virgin, flanked by representations of St. Benedict and St. Scholastica. Other smaller grottoes, containing marble statues, enhance the beauty of this larger work.*

Once this showpiece grotto was finished, the original "Little Jerusalem" miniatures were placed nearby, and the unusual combination of religion and tourism welcomed its first visitors on May 17, 1934. That did not mean it was finished, or that Brother Joseph was ready to prop up his feet and read illuminated texts for the rest of his life. No indeed, for the next twenty-four years he kept building more and more miniatures and placing them in appropriate spots along the walkway that led through the display. Visitors often encountered a stoop-shouldered little man in overalls puttering away in the garden and would ask him who made all the exquisite replicas. He would reply that one of the monks at the abbey was responsible, never giving any hint that he was the artist in question. True to his calling, Brother Joseph never sought credit for himself, even as his creations became more and more famous.

SUPERHIGHWAYS FOR ORDINARY MORTALS

With the number of tourist attractions and amenities increasing, and a corresponding jump in the number of tourists coming to see them, it was more and more obvious that Alabama's highways were quickly becoming obsolete. As we have seen, they were built to carry only a fraction of the amount of traffic that was now bumping along their routes. In fact, at the end of the 1930s, there were many stretches of major federal highways that remained unpaved. Examples included most of U.S. 78 (the former Bankhead Highway) west of Winfield; U.S. 11 from Collinsville to Fort Payne; U.S. 80 from Tuskegee to Phenix City; and nearly all of U.S. 43, which traversed Alabama's western side from Florence to Mobile. In fact, U.S. 31, the "spine" of the state's highways, was one of the few to be paved its entire length in Alabama.

It was bad enough to deal with these narrow, two-lane roads through the countryside—and Alabama certainly had a lot of that—but when tourists had to pass through one of the cities during their journey, it made the situation even worse. One of the most horrendous drives for both out-of-towners and local residents was the stretch of U.S. 11 between Birmingham and Bessemer. Besides the challenges of navigating surface streets in an urban, industrial area, the many railroad crossings in that neighborhood made it seem as if a trip would never be completed. The state highway department came up with a radical plan to literally straighten out the highway mess.

Someone had heard about a highway system in Germany that was known as the Autobahn. Instead of one lane going in each direction, it had at least two and sometimes more. Intersections were carefully designed to move vehicles on and off the highway in an orderly fashion. This farsighted individual convinced the Alabama Highway Department to experiment with building something similar and chose the Birmingham-to-Bessemer jaunt to try it out. On New Year's Day 1936, the *Birmingham News* told its astounded readers that this new, far-fetched idea in travel was about to be a reality:

> *Steam shovels, tractors and wheelbarrows were at work below Powderly on Wednesday as the state and WPA moved to make an actuality out of the long-projected Birmingham–Bessemer super-highway.*
>
> *Characterized as the finest projected highway of its kind in the South, the new super traffic lane will form a picturesque boulevard between the two cities, eliminating curves and speeding the movement of vehicles over a practically "straight shot" route.*
>
> *County Engineer Harry Culverhouse estimated Wednesday the big project will take approximately a year to complete, and involve an expenditure of $1,500,000. While the project is under direction of the State Highway Department, it is listed as a WPA project, and is drawing the major portion of its labor from Uncle Sam's reservoir.*

The Bessemer Superhighway, as it was finally called, was not as much a freeway of the Autobahn model as the highway department had hoped. It did not quite eliminate traffic lights at intersections, nor did it have exits and entrances, but it was still enough of a wonder that many people who were not even going anywhere made the trip between Birmingham and Bessemer just to be able to say they had driven on it. By 1940, it was becoming lined with all the usual tourist necessities, including the Wigwam Village. This was a motor court with cabins shaped like giant concrete tepees, part of a chain begun in Kentucky earlier in the 1930s. A site on the new superhighway being chosen for the chain's only Alabama outlet was a sure sign that it was considered a major passageway for tourists.

A similar approach was tried on the other side of Birmingham, where U.S. 31 left downtown and climbed the steep slope of Red Mountain before plunging down the other side, only to encounter Shades Mountain before continuing its path toward the flat plains of central Alabama toward Montgomery. In February 1941, the *News* described the problem:

> *The treacherous curves and grades on the Montgomery Highway over Shades Mountain have proven a bugaboo to motorists for years, and many tourists avoided the highway because of the extent and danger of the curves. Countless wrecks and many lives were marked up against this highway's record.*
>
> *Now, where once virgin forests stood and hulking boulders discouraged even the most hardened hiker, there is slowly but surely coming into being a sloping, modern and almost awe-inspiring super-highway destined to eliminate one of the most dangerous traffic problems in Alabama.*

While this new alignment of U.S. 31 south of town was being straightened out, another new four-lane thoroughfare that would be known as the Green Springs Highway was being constructed over the mountain a few miles west of U.S. 31. Postcards from the early 1940s show that, at least for a while, the Green Springs Highway was considered an alternate route of U.S. 31, although this does not show up on maps. It was, however, another step in the attempt to get traffic moving more efficiently, but it would be another twenty years or so before an official highway program with that goal would be implemented nationwide.

Vulcan Lives Long and Prospers

As old two-lane U.S. 31 crept across the summit of Red Mountain, in the late 1930s another sight rose above it that would come to be the very symbol of Birmingham and one of the most-visited stopovers on that highway's entire Alabama route. However, the story began almost forty years earlier.

The 1904 World's Fair in St. Louis, in hindsight, was quite remarkable as the birthplace of many future pop culture icons ranging from the ice

In 1939, the 56-foot-tall cast-iron statue of Vulcan was mounted atop a 124-foot pedestal on the crest of Red Mountain, overlooking busy U.S. 31 as it snaked its way from Birmingham to Montgomery.

cream cone to Buster Brown shoes. It was also the debut of a fifty-six-foot-tall statue of Vulcan, the Roman god of fire, cast in iron as the city of Birmingham's demonstration of its steelmaking power. Made from a clay original sculpted by Giuseppe Moretti, Birmingham's Vulcan statue was one of the must-see sights of the fair—but after it was over, it seemed very few people wanted to look at him.

When Vulcan's various pieces were delivered back to the city of his birth, there was no little controversy about what should be done with him. There was a strong sentiment for erecting the giant figure in the main city park downtown, but the society ladies whose homes rimmed the property soon put the kibosh on that idea. There was no doubt that Vulcan was ugly, as that was how he was described and portrayed in Roman mythology, and his bare rear end exposed by his apron did not make him any more socially acceptable.

"The whole history of Vulcan has grown tiresome," one newspaper writer stated. "No one wants to read anything about it, and how very tired people will grow if they are compelled to see it day after day in Capitol Park." Finally, out of desperation, the big lug was assembled (incorrectly, as it turned out) at the Alabama State Fairgrounds alongside U.S. 11, and there he spent the next three decades as a sideshow figure and oversized billboard for various advertisers.

By the mid-1930s, Birmingham had decided that Vulcan deserved better treatment, and plans were drawn up for a park on the crest of Red Mountain, overlooking U.S. 31's serpentine path. The huge statue would be placed atop a 124-foot pedestal, from which he could be seen from nearly any point in the city. With the WPA doing most of the work, the pedestal and grounds were adorned with the sandstone rockwork that was already so familiar, and Vulcan Park had its grand opening on May 8, 1939, with three thousand people in attendance.

At that point, and for many years afterward, practically the only thing to do at Vulcan Park was to climb the 159 stairs inside the pedestal until, somewhat winded, one could stand on the metal observation platform that encircled the pedestal just below the big guy's oversized feet. On the hillside below, leading down to the parking lot, there were cascading fountains stocked with large koi goldfish. Because practically every adult living in Birmingham at the time had been a witness to Vulcan's history, there was no need for a museum or any other exhibit to explain his origins. That would come later, but for the present, Vulcan Park was an impossible-to-ignore sight along the U.S. 31 corridor.

There's a War Going On

Among all the other major tourist routes we have seen so far, there was another that is almost forgotten today. That was U.S. 241, a highway that no longer exists. Let's see how the newspapers described it when it was at its peak:

> *Highway 241 makes a swing from northeastern Alabama over to the central Georgia state line and then cuts back down through southeastern Alabama and then into Florida. Persons living in eastern Tennessee no longer have to go to Birmingham to reach Florida, although there are two Florida routes*

that branch out from Birmingham. One is the Florida Short Route through Sylacauga and the other is the Montgomery–Dothan Highway, better known as the Blue and Gray.

There was much celebration when the final seventeen-mile link of U.S. 241 in Alabama was completed, south of Eufaula to the Henry County line. "It is now possible for persons living in eastern Tennessee to drive to Florida on an all-paved short cut that saves many hours' driving time," reporter Jack House wrote. There was only one little problem that was going to stand in the way of all this promised progress, and it certainly was not the fault of anyone along 241's new route.

In one of those accidents of timing that could not possibly have been worse, the nearly full-page article about 241's completion appeared in the newspaper on Sunday morning, December 7, 1941. (The actual opening ceremony had taken place in Eufaula the previous Thursday.) By the time the day was over, people would have far more pressing matters on their minds, and U.S. 241's reputation as a tourist corridor would have to wait.

Anyone who studies the World War II years will quickly realize how that conflict had an almost devastating effect on tourism on a nationwide scale. Because of the rationing of tires and gasoline, traveling for fun had to be put on hold. In fact, one of the most often-heard slogans of the war years was: "Is this trip really necessary?" Add to this that most families were broken up, with the male members serving in the military or female members doing their important "Rosie the Riveter" work at home, and many roadside businesses that depended solely on travelers had to close up for the duration. Alabama's sites such as Ave Maria Grotto and Bellingrath Gardens survived because they had a healthy source of local visitors, but restaurants, service stations and motels had a particularly hard time of it.

With the outcome of the war so uncertain until almost the end, no one knew what the following years were going to bring. What they did end up bringing for Alabama, though, was a period of tourism prosperity that those few in the industry in 1941 could not have imagined.

Chapter 2
Stepping on the Accelerator

Perhaps the 1950s could be called the golden age of tourism. There were ten years in particular, beginning with the postwar world of 1946, when Americans (and Alabamians) took to the highways for vacation trips that would have been unthinkable before the war. The old federal highways, most of them only two lanes, were clogged with traffic, but along their edges was a dizzying cornucopia of attractions, motels, restaurants, gas stations and souvenir shops. These heady days lasted until approximately 1956, when the hopelessly outdated highways were set to be replaced by the Federal Interstate Highway Program. As we shall see in this chapter, it was great fun while it lasted.

Carrying the Torch for Tourism

When Americans decided to get back on the roads after the austere World War II years, they did so with a vengeance. In fact, before we were very far into the postwar boom, Americans were killing one another with their vehicles in unprecedented numbers. The ever-increasing tourism market was an appealing one to roadside attractions and businesses, but there was a feeling that something needed to be done to be sure more of those tourists remained alive and able to patronize said businesses.

With that thought in mind, in 1946 the Birmingham Jaycees set out to turn the city's most visible attraction into a crusader for highway safety. Someone conceived the idea of placing a neon torch in Vulcan's outstretched right hand; the light would normally glow green, but if there were any traffic fatalities within the city limits, it would burn red for the following twenty-four hours. The torch was constructed and installed by Birmingham's Alabama Neon Sign Company and was lit for the first time on the night of October 23, 1946.

(As an aside, it stayed green for nine days, and when it turned red for the first time, it was not due to an accident involving two automobiles. Instead, a car had struck and killed a pedestrian in downtown Birmingham, proving that there was more than one way to turn a motor vehicle into a deadly instrument.)

While Vulcan was becoming a warning signal for those who drove recklessly, the State of Alabama was working to get even more tourists (either safe or dangerous) into its environs. There was a general consensus that Alabama was missing out on its share of "rolling gold," as the *Birmingham News* called the tourist trade, largely because of the condition of its roads. Ironically, the one that came in for the biggest criticism was the highway over which Vulcan and his new safety torch loomed, U.S. 31. One year after the torch was installed, the *News* analyzed the situation:

> *U.S. 31 in Alabama—a "natural" to Florida—is not shown on maps of the American Automobile Association as an "A-1 fine" road. As a result, AAA tourist bureaus do not route travelers through Alabama. Now comes Tennessee and admits that perhaps it is adding to Alabama's dilemma. Our sister state to the north readily agrees that some 40 miles of U.S. 31 on its side of the line is just as poor as the rest of the highway that runs down into Alabama. But while "lethargic Alabama" permits its share of the motor tourist trade to be re-routed from Nashville through to Georgia, Tennessee is improving U.S. 31.*

This 1947 article hinted at what was going to be the next frontier to conquer for Alabama's budding tourism industry, although there might have been few people who shared the vision expressed by Charles H. Peay, president of the Alabama Motorists Association:

> *"Until now, Tennessee has offered fine roads to Nashville and from that city on into Georgia, where there are some of the finest roads in the South.*

Now they are giving the tourist a second route that will take him into new vacation territory, the Gulf Coast."

Mr. Peay says that the Gulf Coast is growing as a vacation spot for people in the North and Midwest. It will continue to expand during the next six years, when motor tourist travel in the United States is expected to hit an all-time peak, he predicts.

Peay was quoted as adding, "Here we'll be with tourists coming down on both sides of us, and none coming through Alabama because of our poor roads."

Fortifying the Coast

While Alabama dithered about, trying to solve the built-in problem of its built-in highway system, another prediction made by Charles Peay was coming true. The Gulf Coast, encompassing not only Alabama's short stretch but also Mississippi's and especially the Florida Panhandle, was about to enter a period of growth like it had never seen before. There had been some stirrings of activity in the years just before the war interfered, with the formal openings of Florida's Panama City Beach and Pensacola Beach in the late 1930s, but even those future resorts were still taking baby steps in the late 1940s. We have already seen how Alabama's Gulf State Park was part of the first wave of such facilities in 1935, but the town nearest to it, Gulf Shores, was hardly designed to attract huge swarms of tourists.

One thing the Alabama coast had going for it, in addition to beautiful beaches and the Gulf, was history. Mobile Bay had been the focal point of several famous battles, ranging from the War of 1812 to the Civil War, and two huge forts glared at each other across its mouth. They were almost exactly the same age, but Fort Morgan (on the Gulf Shores side of the bay) got to claim the longest lineage, as it had replaced the much older Fort Bowyer. Construction of Fort Gaines (on Dauphin Island, the barrier just south of Mobile that provided the only beach on that side of the bay) began in the early 1820s, with Fort Morgan following only a year or two afterward.

How the two frowning battlements went from protecting against invaders to welcoming tourists took drastically different directions. In 1926, the United States government sold obsolete old Fort Gaines to the City of Mobile to do

The Civil War battlements of Fort Morgan and Fort Gaines, on either side of Mobile Bay, became tourist attractions immediately following World War II. Yes, that's author Tim Hollis behind those shades, and no, this photo was not taken in the 1940s.

with as it wished. Mobile then deeded the relic to the Alabama Department of Conservation, but there was one roadblock to making it available for visitors. Namely, that was that the only way to access Dauphin Island was by boat. Automobile travelers had to wait until 1954, when a three-mile bridge was completed to connect Dauphin Island to the mainland, before its tourism potential began to be realized. According to the website for the island's current development, sand dunes had built up around Fort Gaines in the intervening years, and the walls had to be excavated before people could be expected to see how the place looked.

By contrast, Fort Morgan had remained an active installation for the U.S. military all the way through World War II. At the war's end, the government donated the fort to the state, and work slowly got underway to make it accessible to all who were interested in learning about its history. One of its most famous, if somewhat gory, sights was the permanent bloodstain left by a Confederate soldier during the Battle of Mobile Bay. It seems that the iron

The Story of Alabama Tourism

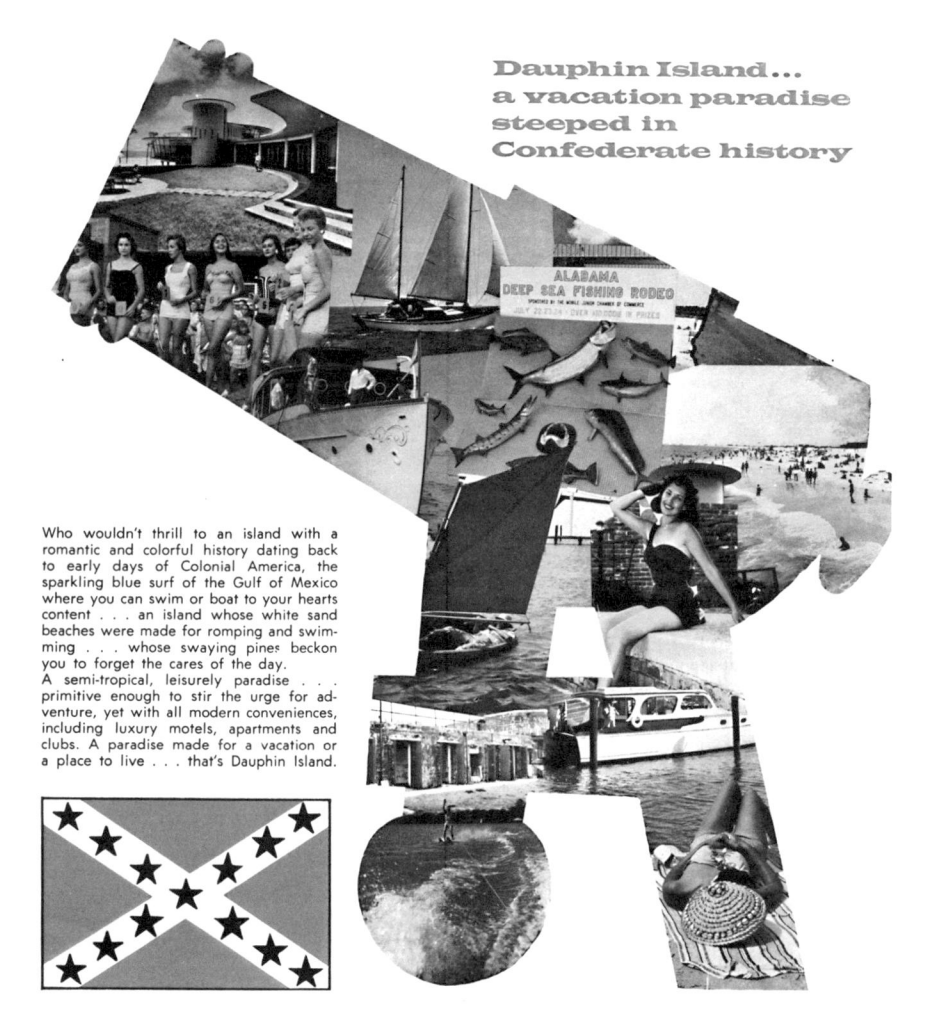

**Dauphin Island...
a vacation paradise
steeped in
Confederate history**

Who wouldn't thrill to an island with a romantic and colorful history dating back to early days of Colonial America, the sparkling blue surf of the Gulf of Mexico where you can swim or boat to your hearts content . . . an island whose white sand beaches were made for romping and swimming . . . whose swaying pines beckon you to forget the cares of the day.
A semi-tropical, leisurely paradise . . . primitive enough to stir the urge for adventure, yet with all modern conveniences, including luxury motels, apartments and clubs. A paradise made for a vacation or a place to live . . . that's Dauphin Island.

Development of Dauphin Island as a tourist destination began in earnest after a bridge from the mainland was constructed in 1954. The inhabitants were clearly proud of their island's role during the War Between the States.

contained in the human blood interacted with the stone from which the fort was built and left a reddish-brown memorial to at least one former resident.

As of Independence Day 1949, getting to Fort Morgan and the seaside communities that adjoined it became a bit easier. That was the date chosen for Governor Jim Folsom to officially open the Gulf Highway, an eleven-mile stretch from Alabama Point on the east to Little Lagoon on the west. Newspapers boasted that "the longtime dream of an Alabama Riviera along

Baldwin County's Gulf of Mexico shoreline is a step nearer reality." The new road passed through Gulf State Park, stopping short of the Alabama-Florida state line—mainly because Florida had not yet built a highway west from Pensacola that would connect with it over Perdido Bay. Gulf Shores, Orange Beach and the other tiny encampments along that highway began preparing to welcome their share of the ever increasingly profitable tourist business, but it would be at least another decade before things began getting really interesting in the neighborhood.

Home-Grown Candy

Whether tourists were headed to the beach or some other vacation spot, they could not be expected to drive for hours and hours without stopping for refreshment or restrooms (not necessarily in that priority). Roadside businesses to serve these needs sprang up along the highways like wildflowers, and one chain of them was Alabama born and Alabama based throughout its entire lifespan.

In 1939, Henry and Cora Saxon began manufacturing candy using the carefully guarded recipes they had inherited from a longtime Birmingham confectioner. Throughout the war years, the Saxons continued to make what limited quantities of candy they could, considering the rationing of sugar and so forth, but in the brave new postwar world, they decided to expand their business exponentially.

In 1947, they opened their first roadside store, known as Saxon's Candy Box, along what was then U.S. 241 at Wellington, just north of Anniston. (That stretch is now part of U.S. 431.) Just as the promoters had promised immediately before the war, U.S. 241 had indeed grown into a major route to Florida for drivers who did not necessarily have a reason to detour through Birmingham and/or Montgomery. The Candy Box became a landmark for so many of those travelers that the Saxons began to entertain thoughts of an entire chain of candy stores.

The Saxon's chain, in its final form, began in 1953. Besides the candy, each location also contained a souvenir shop and a restaurant, making it a one-stop shop for tourists in need of a break from behind the wheel. Before the decade was over, there were nine locations scattered throughout Alabama, with a tenth one just over the state line at Bremen, Georgia. Besides the original Wellington store (which now did double duty as home office and

SAXON'S CANDY KITCHEN
Three Stores
For Your Convenience

U. S. 11 Attalla, Ala.
U. S. 241 Wellington, Ala.
U. S. 231 Harpersville, Ala.

Henry and Cora Saxon began their chain of roadside candy and souvenir stores with a single location at Wellington in 1947. At the time of this promotional card, they had three such shops, but by the 1960s the Saxon's chain would spread throughout Alabama and even into neighboring states.

manufacturing plant for the rest of the chain), the colorful Saxon's signage could be found in Decatur, Albertville, Summit, Pell City, Harpersville, Attalla, Fort McClellan and Pike Road. In true advertising tradition, the billboards promoting each Saxon's store began thirty miles ahead of time, tempting travelers with images of the goodies to be had within, until stopping was almost mandatory.

One might think that the whole story of Saxon's sounds a whole lot like that of a much larger and more legendary chain of roadside businesses: Stuckey's. One would be correct, but the two of them managed to coexist peacefully for many years along Alabama's highways. Stuckey's, as most roadside historians know, had originated in Eastman, Georgia, in 1936, when W.S. Stuckey and his wife began selling their surplus pecans (and candy made from them) in a single small stand. By the time the United States entered World War II, there were three Stuckey's stores, but just as with everyone else in the industry, further growth had to be put on hold to tend to the important business of winning the war. That accomplished, Stuckey's growth during the 1950s was prodigious.

SEE ALABAMA FIRST

PECAN SHOPPE
Stuckey's Grand Opening
Saturday, May 28th
Sunday, May 29th

FREE SAMPLES ON OPENING DAYS

FREE 1-Lb. Box of Peanut Brittle with Every 10 Gallons of Gasoline Purchased Sat. or Sun.

We Specialize In ---

- FINE PECANS
  - PECAN CANDIES
    - TROPICAL JELLIES
      - MARMALADES
        - FANCY GIFT PACKAGES

Hickory Smoked Hams

Souvenirs

Complete Gift Service

Texaco Products

ASK FOR OUR CATALOG

Stuckey's

4 Miles South of Bessemer on New Super Highway U. S. 11

The most famous roadside candy stores of all, Stuckey's, came to Alabama in the 1950s. The earliest locations were along federal highways, but once the interstate system got underway, Stuckey's was a pioneer at establishing outposts at exits far from other necessary amenities.

A 1952 map of Stuckey's locations shows none in Alabama; however, by 1955, the company's official guide indicated two of them, one at Prattville and the other at Loxley. (Amazingly, the Loxley structure still stands today, although it was converted into other retail use many years ago.) That same year, a third Stuckey's opened on the Bessemer Superhighway, just south of Bessemer. At some point, another one appeared on U.S. 231, just north of the Dothan city limits, and yet another on U.S. 280 (the Florida Short Route) at Sylacauga. Stuckey's biggest presence in Alabama, as in most other states where the chain operated, was to accompany the interstate highway program, and we shall revisit that topic in our next chapter.

Saxon's, on the other hand, remained primarily a two- and four-lane-highway institution. It, too, would see changes during the 1960s, so we will also catch up with Henry and Cora once we get down to that part of our story and see what they are up to.

Falling for Noccalula

Near Gadsden, atop the southern end of Lookout Mountain, there was a one-hundred-foot-drop waterfall that had been a familiar sight to residents for more than a century. It had been known as Black Creek Falls, for the waterway whose flow it interrupted, but it became far more famous under its alternate name, which originated in a Cherokee legend of ancient times. It seems there was this princess who was in love with a brave from her own tribe, but her chieftain father was determined that she marry a wealthy chief of the Creek tribe—sort of a Romeo and Juliet in reverse, one might say. Writer and musician Mathilde Bilbro penned the most poetic version of the story, and this is how its climax reads in her rendition:

> *The wedding day came and a great feast was prepared. In silence, Noccalula allowed herself to be arrayed in festive wedding robes. It was incredible! To be sold to a stranger by the father she loved, and her chosen lover forever banished.*
>
> *Noccalula could not go on with it. Overcome with grief, she quietly slipped away from the merrymakers during the festivities. The soft, rhythmical rush of waters called her. For a moment, she stood poised upon the brink of the yawning chasm. One leap—and her troubles were over.*

Heartbroken, the remorseful father gave the great cataract his daughter's name, and since that day the falls have been called NOCCALULA.

Historians have debated for years about the historical accuracy (or lack of same) of this legend, especially inasmuch as practically the same tale is told about a spot at the other extremity of Lookout Mountain, Lover's Leap in Rock City Gardens, with only the names changed to protect the innocent. The main difference is that in that version, Romeo and Juliet live again, and the princess falls in love with a member of an enemy tribe, choosing to end it all rather than give in to her father. There is also a similar legend at Blowing Rock, North Carolina, where this time the male half of the beleaguered romantic couple leaps off the precipice and is magically blown back into his sweet intended's arms by an updraft. Regardless of whether any or all of these stories are true, they seem to indicate that most Native American tribes realized that living in a mountainous area provided a sure-fire way to end it all, should that ever become necessary.

So Black Creek Falls became better known as Noccalula Falls over the decades, but the idea that it should be preserved as a park, and eventually a tourist attraction, was a long time coming. According to historian Danny Crownover, a local resident named Thomas McClung first obtained the falls and forty acres of surrounding property in 1845, later selling the land to G.O. Baker, who bought additional adjoining acreage. The City of Gadsden got interested when it looked like progress was going to mow down Noccalula Falls and its neighborhood with its relentless forward march. Crownover writes:

> *In 1929, while a building boom was on, in and around the city, the late Colonel R.A. Mitchell, banker, industrialist, mayor and town builder, saw that the land overlooking the falls was being plotted into lots for sale to the public. Mitchell also knew there were plans to strip the land of timber. He deplored such proposed destruction of this scenic attraction, and bought the 169 acres surrounding the falls. He decided that this property should be reserved for a city park.*

At least Mitchell's actions kept the falls preserved better than their namesake princess, but the City of Gadsden did not have the necessary funds to purchase the property until 1946. By that time, Mitchell had gone on to join Noccalula in the happy hunting grounds, and his daughter, Sadie Elmore, was in control of the land. In 1949, Gadsden purchased eighty more acres, and local newspapers raved, "The purchase of Noccalula Falls' property is about the best investment the city has ever made."

Getting this chapter back on track with its discussion of the 1950s, it is true that the City of Gadsden made its first tracks in the new Noccalula Falls Park in June 1950, when construction began on restrooms, sewer lines, electric facilities and concession space. Throughout the rest of that decade, picnic facilities and barbecue pits were built, along with a lookout platform over the falls and stairs that led down into the gorge. However, for now we will have to leave it at that because it would be well into the next decade before Noccalula Falls Park became more than just a city park and developed into one of the top tourist draws in Alabama's northern mountains.

The Greater of Two Weevils

One of Alabama's most publicized, and least commercialized, attractions had existed since 1919. That was the year the City of Enterprise erected a monument to the boll weevil, that destructive pest that had decimated the region's cotton crop and forced the citizens to diversify into other (even more profitable) industries. However, for its first thirty years, the monument was simply a Grecian lady holding a chalice above her head, serving as a fountain. As more and more tourists began passing through town, they looked for the famed Boll Weevil Monument but could find nothing about this fountain that had anything to do with its name.

In 1949, Enterprise resident Luther Baker crafted a five-pound boll weevil out of metal and affixed it to the top of the chalice, which by now was no longer spurting water. That original bug overlooked the street below until 1954, when it was replaced by a more realistic copper version forged in Birmingham. Apparently, the new insect found the monument as much to its liking as the cotton crop had been because the ugly bug and its graceful supporting player continue to be the main tourism draw in Enterprise to this day.

Let's Get Organized

During 1951 and 1952, many of the seemingly unrelated pieces of the Alabama tourism puzzle began falling into place, and the basis for a future industry was formed. One of the first glimmers that things were about to get more coordinated was the October 1951 establishment of the Alabama Bureau of Publicity and Information. The state legislature created this new department, giving it "the exclusive power and authority to plan and conduct all state programs of information and publicity designed to attract tourists to Alabama." Thus, what would evolve into today's Alabama Tourism Department was charged with bringing all the previously unrelated elements of the tourism business into an organized whole—but that did not mean it was still unlike herding cats.

Coincidentally, it was also at about the same time that those passing through Alabama, or living there, were faced with a highway element previously unknown: established speed limits. Previously, the guideline for automobile speed was "reasonable and proper," but as anyone who has spent any time at all behind a steering wheel can attest, that definition has many different meanings to many different types of people. The new speed limits made some folks put on the brakes, while for others, the law did not affect what they had been doing all along. In November 1951, the *Birmingham News* editorialized:

> *We are, by and large, a law-abiding people. If the speed limit is set by law at 60 miles an hour for automobile traffic on many of the roads in the state, a vast majority of the state's drivers are going to drive at 60 or less, even if there doesn't happen to be a state highway patrolman in sight.*
>
> *The state's law enforcement officers have been given a new weapon with which to control the reckless driver. But the men who patrol the highways are convinced through experience that 85 percent or more of the people will cooperate fully.*

Let's back the vehicle up and take a look at one particular part of that favorable review of the new speed limits. Did you notice the editorial writer's use of the word "weapon" to describe the power that had been handed to highway patrolmen? Well, as history has proven repeatedly, the problem with any weapon is that it can be beneficial to society if wielded properly, but in the hands of a fiend it can become a menace to all. So it was with the speed limit law, which within three months of its institution created a new roadside attraction known as the "speed trap."

And where do you think this new thorn in tourists' sides would sprout? How about on the heavily traveled Florida Short Route, where folks were likely to be trying to get as many miles on the speedometer as possible on the way to those white sands and turquoise waters? Harpersville was one of

The Story of Alabama Tourism

Yachting is popular at Alabama's Gulf Coast.

For Vacations, Visit

ALABAMA

To Our Guests:

On behalf of the citizens of Alabama, I extend to you a most cordial welcome to our State.

As you journey from our great lakes and mountains in North Alabama to our beautiful Gulf of Mexico beaches, and view our many historic shrines and our ante-bellum homes, drive safely and enjoy yourselves.

James E. Folsom, Governor

DeSoto State Park, Near Fort Payne

DRIVE AS YOU WOULD HAVE THE OTHER FELLOW DRIVE

This attractive ad, promoting Alabama's variety from the beaches to the mountains, could be found on the back of the official 1958 state highway map.

51

the first cities along that stretch of highway to discover that there was gold in "them thar travelers," and the speed limit abruptly dropped to twenty-five miles per hour in its corporate limits.

By February 1952, the Alabama Motorists' Association was having to deal with multiple complaints of Harpersville patrolmen stopping out-of-towners and collecting arbitrary amounts of money on the spot, with the promise that they would not have to come back to appear in court. "We are going to stop the collection of money from motorists on the highways anywhere this practice occurs in Alabama," Alabama Motorists' Association officer W.B. Timmons told the press, and Harpersville's city officials ultimately agreed. No police officer would be permitted to collect a fine directly from a driver. In years to come, small towns along many of Alabama's state and federal highways would find a rich source of income by unexpectedly lowering the speed limit and posting a patrolman to catch those who missed such information, but at least we have seen that such a questionable practice is as old as the concept of a speed limit itself.

The condition of the highways on which those drivers were or were not obeying the speed limit was a continuing source of concern. In a state-published report from the late 1940s, the statistics were given that the State Highway Department had jurisdiction over 7,000 miles of highways. Of those, 5,879 miles were paved, 775 miles were "temporarily surfaced all-weather roads" and the remaining 346 miles had yet to be improved (i.e., they were dirt roads). Looming just as large was the problem that, apart from such prewar projects as the Bessemer Superhighway and Green Springs Highway, many of the most-traveled tourist routes were still winding, two-lane affairs that were ill suited to the needs of 1950s travelers.

In December 1951, a state bond issue resulted in voters approving new funds for road improvement. Reading the subsequent news coverage of the highways that were first in line for this project tells a lot about just which ones were considered the most crucial for tourists. As usual, U.S. 31 was one of the first concerns, especially the part from Birmingham to Shelby County, described as "narrow and dangerously winding" and "one of the greatest—and most dangerous—bottlenecks in the entire state highway system." In the other direction, 31 was to be four lane through Cullman County and into Hartselle.

Just because the Bessemer Superhighway served as U.S. 11's route southwest of Birmingham did not mean the rest of it could not stand improving. Plans called for widening U.S. 11 all the way from the end of the Superhighway to Bucksville. It was noted that once 11 crossed into Tuscaloosa County, it

HAUNTED CASTLE

Not a theme park ride, the "Haunted Castle" was actually the ruins of the old Saunders mansion near Courtland, built shortly before the Civil War. It became a hotbed of ghostly activity and was supposedly abandoned quite suddenly by its owners during the 1920s, with later explorers finding their half-finished dinner on the table. Regardless of its historical or supernatural significance, it was allowed to deteriorate into the ruins pictured on this postcard, and what was left of it was demolished in 1961.

was practically wide enough to qualify as a four lane already. "Not only is it wide, smooth and straight, but it has no dangerous turns or other hazards," the article said.

U.S. 78 was to be four lane east of Birmingham, headed toward Leeds. The Florida Short Route was on the list too, even though it would be many years before it eliminated the beautiful, yet somewhat risky, curve known as "The Narrows." This portion, with high cliffs on both sides of the highway and a roaring stream on one of those sides, had to have been one of the most unusual sights for folks on their way to Florida.

All the talk about improving existing highways also created some shifts in their numbering system. In the early 1950s, the official designation for the Florida Short Route changed from Alabama Highway 91 to U.S Highway 280. At about the same time, U.S. 241, which had received so much ill-timed fanfare on the day of the Pearl Harbor attack, was decommissioned; parts of it were designated U.S. 431 and others made part of the new U.S. 280. Drivers who lived in Alabama or who planned to pass through the

SEE ALABAMA FIRST

Travelers from the north who were heading toward Florida got one of the more unusual experiences of their long drive when the stretch of U.S. 280 known as The Narrows twisted and turned through the hills and along a flowing stream southeast of Birmiingham.

54

state certainly needed a constant supply of road maps from their favorite service station in order to keep up with all the rapid changes in routing, road conditions and numbering.

Old Times Here Are Not Forgotten

Perhaps it was merely a coincidence—but probably not—that the 1950s saw the simultaneous beginnings of the civil rights movement in the South and a concentrated effort to establish monuments to the Confederacy. In several Alabama cities, this translated into turning the best-preserved local antebellum mansions into museums that would exemplify the best (but never the worst) of the pre–Civil War era.

No thanks to General Sherman's troops, there were still a number of such mansions scattered throughout the state, so finding them was not much of a problem. Ironically, the biggest city in Alabama—Birmingham—was at a bit of a disadvantage because it did not exist until years after the war ended. However, near Birmingham's ancestor, Elyton, there was a former plantation home that had been built in 1842 and had been a headquarters for the Union troops that had made inroads into that part of Confederate territory. About twenty years after the end of the conflict, it acquired its permanent name: Arlington.

From then until the early 1950s, it remained a private residence. However, in the summer of 1952, owners Mr. and Mrs. A.C. Montgomery (who had lived there since 1924) decided to put the house and its six and a half acres up for sale. There was an immediate reaction from various Birminghamians for the city to purchase the property and turn it into a "shrine to the Confederacy" (no need to mince words there!). All of this was accomplished, and Arlington became Birmingham's memorial to a past that many people were desperately trying to force on the present.

Down in Mobile, where antebellum mansions were as numerous as the azalea bushes that bloomed every spring and the hoop-skirted southern belles who strolled among them, the city picked out a particular one called Oakleigh for its preservation efforts. Built in 1833, the house was described in its tourist literature as "more than just a beautiful period house museum. It's a mood. An atmosphere. The memory of an era gone by, painstakingly preserved amidst the bustling world of the 20th century."

"House museums," a term the Oakleigh advertising employed, became an important subset in the tourism world, even when they were not

SEE ALABAMA FIRST

STANDARD OIL

BIRMINGHAM
AND VICINITY
ROAD MAP

Arlington, restored ante-bellum home.
SEE INFORMATION FOR SIGHT-SEERS

In 1952, the City of Birmingham took great pride in restoring Arlington, the only remaining antebellum home in the immediate area. Its manicured grounds made the cover of a Standard Oil map of the Birmingham vicinity a few years later.

Confederate memorials. Not far from Oakleigh, on the highway leading from Mobile to Bellingrath Gardens, there was the Treasure House (no relation to Captain Kangaroo's TV abode). Here the emphasis was on the contents, rather than the building itself, which included such priceless antiques as a desk that once belonged to Napoleon and a rug that was woven during the reign of Louis XIV. There was even a set of four tapestries woven in France in 1806, depicting scenes from some of that country's most famous fairy tales, including "Cinderella" and "Puss in Boots." As the brochures made perfectly clear:

> *Nothing is for sale, but everything in the Treasure House is open for your leisurely inspection, in order that you and many others may thrill to the beauty of a collection once enjoyed by its owners and their guests.*

Besides Arlington and Oakleigh, there were plenty of other antebellum residences that were turned into attractions of one type or another. Among these were Magnolia Grove (Greensboro), Sturdivant Hall (Selma), Teague House (Montgomery), Gaineswood (Demopolis), the Shorter Mansion (Eufaula), the Gorgas Home (Tuscaloosa) and White Columns (Camden). Even this list is by no means complete.

One of Alabama's most famous house museums was indeed of antebellum vintage, but it was a relatively simple clapboard affair, not a white-columned mansion of the type so beloved by Old South aficionados. In fact, its fame as a tourist attraction was not derived from the house but from the family who lived there—one particular member, to be precise. For that house near Tuscumbia was Ivy Green (accurately named for one of its most prominent landscaping features), and in 1880 it was the birthplace of Helen Keller.

No biography of Helen Keller is needed here, as practically anyone reading this book already knows enough of her story to put Ivy Green into context. After being stricken by some now-unidentifiable disease at age two, Keller was left blind and deaf and, consequently—or so it was believed—unable to speak. However, thanks to her teacher Anne Sullivan, Keller learned to understand the concept of speech and eventually to speak for herself. Not only that, but she also became a world-renowned author, proving that anyone can overcome any obstacle they might find in their path.

Ivy Green became a tourist attraction in 1954, while Keller was still alive. Meticulously preserved, it highlighted the various spots that were important in her life and career, including her bedroom and the pump where Anne Sullivan had made her first breakthrough, teaching her student the word "water."

Tuscumbia's Ivy Green, the birthplace of renowned author and speaker Helen Keller, was opened as an attraction in 1954, during the "First Lady of Courage's" lifetime.

Not many historical tourist attractions could boast personal visits by the individuals they commemorate, but Helen Keller (far right) made periodic visits back to her old home at Ivy Green.

Of all the attractions in Alabama, Ivy Green certainly gained a distinction by being the only one to serve as the setting for a Broadway play. William Gibson's drama *The Miracle Worker* debuted in New York in the fall of 1959, and as the *Birmingham News* was quick to point out, all of the action in the play, except for one brief scene, took place at Ivy Green. In the original production, Anne Bancroft and Patty Duke starred as Anne Sullivan and Helen Keller, respectively, and the critics raved. The play was made into a movie in 1962, and to this day, it is performed several times annually at Ivy Green. Although Keller cannot honestly be said to have ever "seen" *The Miracle Worker*, or even heard its dialogue, she was well aware of it and continued to make occasional visits to Tuscumbia until her death in 1968.

It's All Natural

Ask just about any veteran tourist from east of the Mississippi River where Natural Bridge is, and they will immediately say, "In Virginia, of

Virginia was not the only state to have a Natural Bridge Park. Alabama had one, too, and this souvenir plate was one of many, many different souvenirs offered that bore its name and image.

course." It is true that Virginia's Natural Bridge has been an attraction since the days when it was operated by none other than Thomas Jefferson, but it certainly had no monopoly on that type of rock formation. Alabama had one, too, between Jasper and Haleyville in Winston County, and it was said to be the longest "natural bridge" east of the Rocky Mountains. Besides that, Alabama's was actually made up of two rock bridges paralleling each other, so that gave it something else to brag about.

In 1954, Albert Day Legg of Jasper opened Natural Bridge Park surrounding this ancient site, and to this day the park makes it perfectly clear that very little has been added to supplement the natural beauty—picnic tables, restrooms and a souvenir shop being about the extent of it. Oh yes, "Natural Bridge of Alabama" souvenirs abound in antique stores, proving just how many visitors Legg's park has attracted over the decades. Besides the titular Natural Bridge, the property also contained many other formations that were given whimsical names, faintly echoing the theme of Lookout Mountain's Rock City Gardens.

Alabama's Natural Bridge Park contained not only the titular geologic feature but some human-enhanced visual gags along its trail as well.

The resemblance between Natural Bridge and Rock City did not end there. Natural Bridge employed, as its primary form of outdoor advertising, signs painted on the roofs and walls of barns and country stores throughout that section of Alabama. Perhaps they never attained the sheer legendary reputation of the "See Rock City" barns, but "See Natural Bridge" signs were certainly a familiar enough sight to those who traveled in and around Walker and Winston Counties.

(Natural Bridge's only real rival in this form of advertising was the Western Auto store in Dora, which also employed sign painters to emblazon its name on rooftops and walls and, when neither was available, sometimes on the sheer rock faces of cliffs alongside the highways. Occasionally, a rusting "Dora Western Auto" sign can still be discerned on abandoned buildings on back roads of the region.)

The northwestern quadrant of Alabama seemed to be an incredibly fertile spot for attractions of Natural Bridge Park's type. Not far away, at Hodges, Rock Bridge Canyon was offering practically the same sights, including another of "one of the nation's largest natural bridges," according to the signage. Like Natural Bridge Park, Rock Bridge Canyon had other named features, including Echo Rock, Turtle Rock, Ten Commandments Rock, Hidden Cave, Spy Rock and Noah's Ark.

But wait, there's more! Only a couple of miles from Rock Bridge Canyon, near Hackleburg, one could spend a cheery day at Dismals Wonder Gardens (sometimes shortened to just Dismals Gardens), another woodland tour through strange rock formations—but no natural bridge, for once. Never mind, because where else could one see wind- and water-carved stone heads of a Native American chief and princess, plus a rock lion, Witch's Cave and Fat Man's Squeeze? (Oh, okay, Rock City had Fat Man's Squeeze, too, but that wasn't in Alabama.) Dismals Gardens' brochure picturesquely described some of the park's other most distinguishing features:

> *During the warm season the rarest phenomenon of all occurs when the dripping rocks are aglow at night with myriads of tiny phosphorescent worms that twinkle like the stars above. Never explained, not found elsewhere, they are called Dismalites.*
>
> *In three places, phantom waterfalls add to the mystery and dream-like atmosphere. The ear responds, but not the eye.*

None of these attractions made a gigantic impression in the overall story of Alabama tourism, although the town of Natural Bridge at least named itself after its most prominent feature. As of 2002, the community's official population was given as somewhere between twenty-nine and forty-nine, with the Natural Bridge Restaurant as the biggest employer. The others have simply maintained their steadfast, rock-like demeanor, unchanging as the tourism world around them continued to morph into new and different forms.

Cave Men

Not all the rocky sights to be seen were above ground. There was another world underneath, and northern Alabama's mountainous terrain meant there was a lot of that world to explore. Two of the state's premier "show caves" opened during the 1950s, with more to come in the decades that followed. None, of course, could strictly be defined as a "new" attraction, but each attracted a lot of attention with its belated entrance onto the tourism stage.

In the early 1950s, Eddie Rickles and his troop of Boy Scouts did their good deed for the day by discovering a cave near Hayden. That is, if you can call it a "discovery" when locals had known about it since the 1890s. The point was that no one in all those years had thought to make a roadside

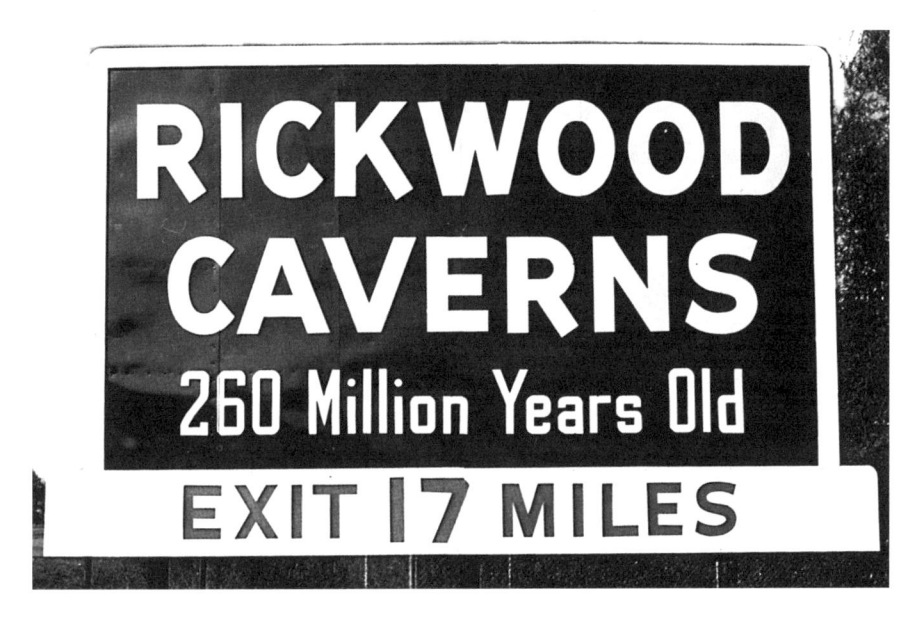

Rickwood Caverns, near Warrior, was one of the most aggressive roadside advertisers in the state. Its red-and-white billboards could be found along main highways and country back roads alike.

attraction out of this cave, so Rickles took on a partner, Sonny Arwood, and set about to open it to the public. What to call it? It had no preexisting name, so Rickles and Arwood combined pieces of their own monikers and advertised their new attraction as Rickwood Caverns.

Beginning with its opening in 1954, Rickwood Caverns gave Natural Bridge Park and Dora Western Auto some competition in the roadside advertising race. Rickwood did not employ rooftops nearly as often as those two enterprises—probably because they snatched up most of the suitable ones!—but neither could come close to Rickwood's sheer number of billboards. The red-and-white metal signs were particularly thick along U.S. 31, the nearest federal highway to its entrance, but they could also be found along country roads and in farmland all over the northern half of Alabama.

At about the same time, another cave was being discovered (for the second or third or fourth time) at Grant, north of Guntersville. The story of its development into an attraction was documented by no less prestigious a publication than *Reader's Digest*, which introduced its readers to Huntsville newspaper writer Don Fulton and Redstone Arsenal employee Jay Gurley and invited them to digest the story of Cathedral Caverns.

After Cathedral Caverns, near Grant, opened in the summer of 1959, it soon became famous for the sheer size and scope of its underground formations, including the largest-known cave entrance anywhere.

The saga went like this:

> One bright July morning in 1952, Gurley and Fulton had come to forsaken Gunter Mountain, eleven miles from a highway and a mile walk from the end of the nearest rural lane. At first they didn't see the cave's tree-screened entrance. Then, feeling a draft, they followed the cool air through the brush—and walked into the biggest cave mouth either of them had ever seen. Arching 40 feet high and 128 feet wide, it looked big enough to swallow New York's Grand Central terminal.

The two spelunkers continued exploring the cave, and six hours into their journey they discovered a wall with other people's names and dates, proving that they were not exactly breaking new ground. The farther they went, though, the less graffiti they saw, until they knew they were now where no man had gone before.

Of the two, Gurley was the most obsessed with the idea of opening the cave to the public, and he hocked practically everything he owned to buy the land and have trails constructed and lighting installed. By the summer of 1959, Cathedral Caverns—named for its largest expanse, the Cathedral Room—was ready for visitors. It and Rickwood Caverns proved that people were just as willing to spend their money to tramp about underground as to play and frolic on top of it, and a new sub genre of Alabama attraction was established.

THE NATION'S INNKEEPER

With seemingly at least one new attraction opening every year, the need for dependable food and lodging along Alabama's highways was growing exponentially. Mom and pop restaurants and motels were still the most common, but stopping at one of them could sometimes be a bit like playing Russian roulette, as a traveler could never be sure just what sort of experience he would encounter. This partly explains the rise of chain restaurants, which seem to have been quite late in coming to Alabama. Howard Johnson's was probably the first, having raised its orange roof in Birmingham by 1954, with one location on U.S. 78 at the eastern end of the city limits and another on U.S. 11, at just about the spot where it became the Bessemer Superhighway. That four-lane thoroughfare was also going to be the birthplace for the chain motel industry in the state.

In 1952, a Memphis businessman named Kemmons Wilson had set out to do for the lodging industry what Howard Johnson's had done for restaurants: create a chain that people who traveled across the country could recognize from city to city and have enough confidence to patronize it over and over. Wilson's architect drew up the first plans and, inspired by the 1942 Bing Crosby movie he had watched on television the night before, scrawled the name "Holiday Inn" on his rendering. Wilson liked it, and once the original Holiday Inn in Memphis was open, he began trying to sell franchises for other cities.

Richard Hail Brown of Birmingham attended one of Wilson's early franchise seminars, and while there were not many other takers for such a revolutionary idea at the time, Brown plunked down $500 to buy a Holiday Inn franchise for Birmingham and all of Jefferson County. He chose to build his new project between Birmingham and Bessemer, just south of the veteran—but considered antiquated—Wigwam Village. An article about his new Holiday Inn specified that he felt Bessemer needed a suitable place to host conventions and sales meetings, as well as a quality restaurant. Because the iron and steel industry was still roaring at full blast, Brown hoped his modern "motor hotel" would attract the out-of-town dignitaries who frequently visited their interests in the area.

Brown's Holiday Inn opened in the summer of 1954 and immediately attracted attention from across the state because no one had ever seen such a luxurious motel. Its conveniences more closely resembled what one might find in a downtown hotel, which was the whole idea. To be honest, it does sound as if Alabama's first Holiday Inn was a bit more elaborate than most

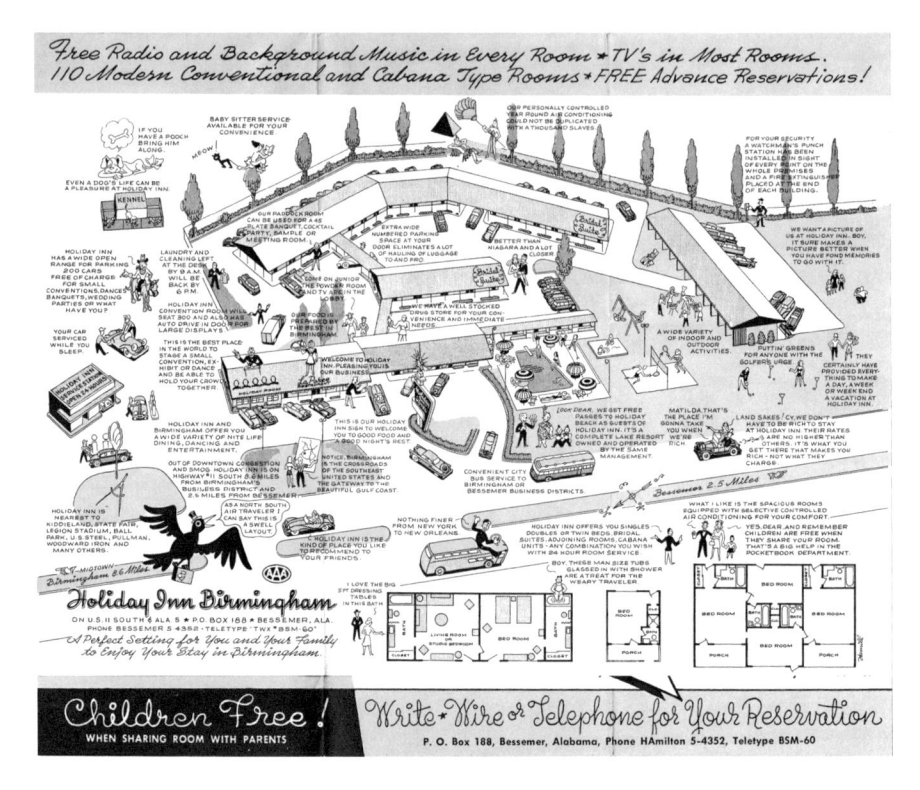

Memphis-based Holiday Inn was just getting a toehold along the nation's highways when its first location in Alabama opened on U.S. 11, between Birmingham and Bessemer, in the summer of 1954. As one can tell from this brochure's map of the property, no effort or expense was spared to make sure a Holiday Inn was more than just another collection of tourist cabins.

later installments in the chain, containing eighty-two rooms (later enlarged), a Mary Ball candy shop, a lounge, a library, a drugstore, a barbershop, a gift shop, a beauty parlor, an assembly hall, a twenty-four-hour service station and the aforementioned restaurant, operated as a branch of downtown Birmingham's famed La Paree. Of course, the front lawn featured a swimming pool underneath the now-iconic Holiday Inn "Great Sign," as it was known within the company. Since people had yet to learn what a Holiday Inn was, it was one of the few signs that actually contained the word "Hotel" in addition to the famous script logo.

At the same time Brown was building his motel, he was also embarking on another tourist-related project a few miles south of Bessemer on U.S. 11. Known as Holiday Beach, the park did market itself to tourists but was primarily a getaway spot for locals who were unwilling or financially unable to make a trip to the Gulf Coast. Holiday Beach had a lake with its own white sandy shore and other entertainment features.

Brown sold his Bessemer Holiday Inn in 1957, but the family is still in the motel consultation business today. In the 1960s, Brown started his own chain of motels known as Hiway Host, each of which had yet another eye-grabbing neon sign shaped like the U.S. federal highways shield. Hiway Hosts could soon be found across Alabama and into the neighboring states.

Meanwhile, Holiday Inn continued to thrive in Alabama even after Brown left it in other hands. By the time of the company's 1958 directory, the chain was represented in the state with locations in Opelika (at the intersection of U.S. 280 and State Highway 147), Huntsville (on U.S. 231) and Montgomery (on the U.S. 31 South bypass). The big news was that in July 1958, a new "Holiday Inn Riviera Luxury Resort" would be opening on Dauphin Island, yet another step in making that formerly obscure sand spit a major force in Alabama's beaches.

Superhighways on Steroids

That nagging problem remained of just how to improve the highways that were supposed to deliver travelers to all these new motels and the attractions that awaited nearby. In the spring of 1956, Congress approved the Federal Interstate Highway Program, based largely on Germany's Autobahn system, which President Eisenhower had observed during his time there during World War II. (As we have seen, some highway engineers had already tried to duplicate the Autobahn model in various states, including Alabama, but with uneven and often incomplete results.) Once the money was approved—initially $27 billion—work could begin, and early estimates were that the entire national system of interstate highways would be complete within thirteen years. Okay, you can go ahead and laugh now.

In September 1956, work began on what was planned to be nine hundred miles of interstate highways in Alabama. It was going to be no small task, as itemized by a newspaper account:

> *As now authorized, the new highway system in Alabama includes U.S. 31 from the Tennessee line south through Birmingham and Montgomery to Mobile; U.S. 11 from Chattanooga to Meridian; U.S. 78 from*

Monkey Island was the first phase of what would eventually become Birmingham's Jimmy Morgan Zoo in 1955. The attraction is now known simply as the Birmingham Zoo, and the monkeys and their moat have given way to more modern zoological exhibits.

> *Birmingham to Atlanta; U.S. 80 across middle Alabama from state line to state line; U.S. 90 across Baldwin County to Mobile; and U.S. 29, the Montgomery–Atlanta Highway.*

At this early stage in the game, it is interesting to note that only the established federal highway numbers were used. The new interstate numbers that would come to replace them had apparently not yet been decided on, or else it was thought the public might be confused by them. It is also notable that U.S. 78 was described as being part of the new system only from Birmingham toward Atlanta. The other half of 78 in Alabama, the part that passed through John H. Bankhead's former stomping grounds, was left out of the plans. In fact, without getting too far ahead of our story, it would be well into the twenty-first century before an interstate highway eased the traffic problems through northwest Alabama.

(As a sort of consolation prize, in the summer of 1957 plans were drawn up to build a new four-lane route for 78 between Birmingham and the Walker County line. Even though some additional work was done over the next fifty years, there are still many areas north of Jasper, heading toward the Mississippi state line, where the route of old 78/Bankhead Highway is still two lanes, as it always was.)

The next time someone asks you a trivia question about where the first interstate construction in Alabama took place, you will be all set to win the prize because you are reading this book. That initial work consisted of five miles of U.S. 31 between Kimberly and Warrior. It was considered revolutionary because instead of passing through Warrior, it bypassed the town on its western side. This method of routing interstates would have far-reaching effects on the attractions and businesses that had set up shop over the previous fifty years. (Ironically, even though it was publicized as the first segment of Alabama's interstate system, those five miles remained a part of U.S. 31.)

The next plan called for an even longer stretch of interstate bypassing Blount Springs, Hanceville and Cullman, straightening out a huge curve made by U.S. 31 as it twisted through all those towns. Toward the south, similar construction was planned to pull traffic around, instead of through, Clanton for those headed toward Montgomery and the Gulf Coast. Of course, all the other highways were in line for improvements too, but some were further back in line than others. Here are some bits and pieces of those plans:

> *Plans are not complete for the route of U.S. 78 East, but chances are that the new four-lane construction to a point near Leeds will be accepted as a part of the route after intersections are eliminated by overpasses, underpasses, etc.*
>
> *Apparently much of U.S. 11 between Birmingham and Chattanooga will have to be reworked. On U.S. 11 south of Birmingham, authorities have agreed that the present four-lane construction is not adaptable to the new route. Whatever route is decided, it will extend to the end of the present four-lane construction south of Bessemer.*
>
> *Surveys are not complete concerning the route of U.S. 11 south from Vance to Eutaw. In all probability, the route will pass close enough to link Tuscaloosa by relatively short "access" or feeder roads.*
>
> *On U.S. 29 between Montgomery and Atlanta, it has been decided to build four-lane construction bypassing the present four-lane route between*

Interstate 65

When was the last time anyone thought of enshrining an interstate on a postcard? At the time this one was produced, such superhighways were still something of a novelty. Most of the publicity seemed directed toward I-65, which ran the entire length of Alabama from the Tennessee state line to Mobile.

> *Auburn and Opelika. Authorities have not agreed as to the method for reaching Mobile on U.S. 90. It could be that the superhighway will span the Mobile River by a new and more direct bridge if the Bankhead Tunnel under the river is not taken over.*

Eventually, the interstate highway numbers were revealed. I-65 would parallel the route of U.S. 31; I-20 would replace the part of U.S. 78 east of Birmingham and would also run into Tuscaloosa; I-59 would follow U.S. 11's route down from Chattanooga, overlapping with I-20 until the two separated again in Mississippi; I-10 would replace U.S. 90's brief trek across Baldwin and Mobile Counties; and I-85 would be the new link between Montgomery and Atlanta. These names would come to be so familiar to drivers that many people tend to forget that the old highways are still there, until construction or a major wreck shuts down the interstates and forces everyone to seek alternate routes.

The Past Meets the Future

Just before the 1950s gasped their last, another couple of attractions opened that represented two very different approaches. One had its feet mired firmly in the past, while the other was reaching into the future—only it didn't know it.

As for the first one, in June 1957 the boundaries were approved for the new Horseshoe Bend National Military Park near Dadeville. As most of those who studied Alabama history in elementary school know, Horseshoe Bend (a sharp curve in the Tallapoosa River) was the site of an epic battle between General Andrew Jackson and the Creek Indians in 1814. By 1957, most of the surrounding property was owned by Alabama Power, but the Department of the Interior managed to swing a deal with Reddy Kilowatt to obtain most of it. Adjoining property was acquired over the next few years, ensuring that it would never become the site of the Horseshoe Bend Walmart, for example.

Meanwhile, at Alabama's northern extremity, Huntsville was beginning to be known as "Rocket City" by virtue of the work being done at Redstone Arsenal. By 1958, colorful postcards were describing the arsenal in these terms:

> *This is the research and development center for rockets and guided missiles. Here has centered the development of the Nike-Ajax, Nike-Hercules, Corporal, Sergeant, Hawk, Dart, Little John, Honest John, Lacrosse, Hermes, Redstone, Jupiter and Jupiter C, which launched America's first earth satellite.*

In case none of those names mean a thing to you, realize that at this stage Redstone Arsenal's work was considered more a matter of defense during the Cold War than Huntsville's later fame for preparing to explore the final frontier. In the late 1950s and early '60s, Americans were more interested in preserving what they had on earth than they were in blasting off into outer space, and when Russia managed to get a working satellite (Sputnik) into the wild blue yonder first, it came close to giving the good old USA an inferiority complex.

To prove to everyone that America was inferior to no one, Redstone Arsenal opened portions of its property to tourists and displayed some of its proudest creations. For a while, the exhibits were housed in a huge dome, 150 feet in diameter and 85 feet high, painted to resemble a globe. It was touted

Hard as it is to believe, crude displays such as this one at Redstone Arsenal near Huntsville were the larval stage of one of the top attractions in the state: the Space and Rocket Center.

Another embryonic version of Huntsville's famed space center was this Redstone Arsenal "Pentadomes" complex that housed miniature models of rockets and missiles.

as "the largest space museum in the world," a prophetic statement if there ever was one. Other oversized missiles were scattered around a public picnic area to reassure Americans and frighten enemy agents. As one postcard put it so succinctly, "Sights like this provide a feeling of safety and security that you can't purchase with a can of insecticide."

REST STOP

The Warrior River Motel, on U.S. 78 south of Jasper, was a typical single-story 1950s example of its type of lodging. In the inset photo, notice the country store across the street with a painted rooftop advertising Natural Bridge Park. *Dixie Neon collection.*

See Alabama First

Top: Natural Bridge Park was not the only way that rock formation helped the local economy. A motel and restaurant also capitalized on the visitors who came to the area.

Left: On U.S. 31, just south of Birmingham, the Vulcan Motor Lodge sat within view of the genuine iron statue that inspired its name.

Opposite, top: The Pine Lake Motel, at last report, still operates on U.S. 231 as that busy tourist route makes its way from Montgomery to Florida. Notice that at this point, those staying at the Pine Lake could take advantage of a Saxon's store and restaurant next door.

Opposite, bottom: As the first Holiday Inn in Alabama, the luxurious location at Bessemer knew one of the best ways to attract businessmen and steel tycoons who happened to find themselves in the area. *Mike Cowart collction.*

The Story of Alabama Tourism

In the days before a fast-food restaurant could be found on nearly every corner, motels usually had their own restaurants on the properties. This Pell City establishment is a fine example of that mostly vanished tradition.

Chapter 3
Putting the Pedal to the Metal

When one thinks of the 1960s in Alabama, the many tragic and historical events surrounding the civil rights movement most immediately come to mind. However, believe it or not, those activities would not have any major effect on the state's tourism industry for nearly thirty years after they took place. There is little to no evidence that they had any bearing on the attractions that lined Alabama's highways during the 1960s. In fact, if you thought the tourist business was booming during the previous decade, just grab some snacks and get ready. This is about to be a very long chapter.

Be Careful What You Wish For

At the beginning of 1960, it looked like the interstate highway system in Alabama just might have a chance of delivering on its promise, and within a reasonable time frame. However, as with the bits and pieces of work being done along U.S. 31, interstate construction did not begin at Point A and proceed to Point B in a linear fashion. Instead, as various segments were finished, drivers were obliged to get off the interstate and back on, or off the old highway and onto the interstate, at a sometimes confusing pace.

For example, let's take a newspaper writer's description of one of the interstate's primary features that was thought to be totally unfamiliar:

Here and there, not far from the old familiar highway trails, skyscraper-like concrete frameworks are rearing upward. These will be tomorrow's "interchanges"—differing types and geometric patterns of lines looping and weaving into the new highway from older and lesser routes.

Take the now developing interchange on U.S. 31, some six miles south of Clanton, for instance. It will bind together the present U.S. 31, a newly completed bypass around Clanton, and the new interstate route known as Route No. 65.

As we saw in the last chapter, there was not going to be an interstate to replace every one of the former main tourist routes, and in those cases, there was sometimes work to be done to at least try to bring them closer to the new, modern standard. In April 1960, work began to build a new four-lane U.S. 280 (still known as the Florida Short Route). It would take several years to finish, but once it was done, the picturesque but dangerous two-lane strip through The Narrows would no longer be a necessity. It would, however, still be there for those who chose to navigate its twists and turns because they wanted to.

It was still the interstates that were on everyone's minds, though, and the one that seemed to get more attention than all the rest combined was I-65. This was only natural since it was by far the longest stretch in the state, and it connected Birmingham to Mobile via Montgomery. (Somehow, Huntsville got left out of the picture and had to rely on a spur built decades later.) There was much celebrating when twenty-five miles of I-65 opened the Saturday after Thanksgiving 1960, just in time for the annual Alabama-Auburn football game at Birmingham's Legion Field. Those twenty-five miles cut off a lot of U.S. 31 from four miles south of Clanton to two miles north of Calera.

It was enough to make people drool for more. Another section of I-65 opened in March 1961, leaving only fifteen miles of non-interstate travel between Birmingham and Montgomery. Unfortunately, that's where things seemed to stall, as well into the 1970s tourists bound for Florida still had to get off the unfinished interstate north of Prattville and negotiate U.S. 31 before rejoining the freeway several miles south. In fact, some of the biggest flies in the interstate ointment were the large cities the new superhighways were supposed to connect. With few exceptions, the interstates would zip along for miles and miles, but then as they approached Birmingham or Montgomery, they would run out of gas, leaving surface streets as the only way to get to where one was going.

By the early 1960s, the slow but steady progress of the interstate highways was having an effect on the businesses along the older federal routes. Concerned business owners in central Alabama erected these billboards to encourage drivers to take U.S. 31 instead of its slicker descendant, I-65.

However, those communities in between, which had been well and truly bypassed, often wished they could have had that problem. By June 1961, the changing traffic pattern was already beginning to have a negative effect on businesses and entire towns that had once counted on tourists to keep them alive. *Birmingham News* correspondent Boone Aiken set out on a journey from Autauga County to Thorsby to document the good and the bad of the new highway system. She was particularly shocked by what had happened to the myriad fruit stand operators along U.S. 31. "During one brief stretch, I counted ten fruit stands—nine of them closed," she wrote. "During the trip I saw 21 closed stands, six open for business, and one customer."

Motels were also hurting. Aiken spoke with Mr. and Mrs. Doyle Walker, owners of the D&O Motel in Thorsby. They, too, had a sad story to tell: "The night before the new highway opened, we had a full house. We haven't had one since. Last night, a car passed about every 30 minutes. This time last June, over 100 cars would go by in that time."

As for restaurants, they were going rather hungry, too. The Cloverleaf Motel at Clanton had a connected restaurant, but after the opening of I-65, that adjunct was closed. The Dairy Queen at Clanton also found more of its curly topped ice cream cones on its hands than it used to, but at least businesses such as that one could rely on local customers and not just tourists. Some business owners whistled past the graveyard by opining that the interstate was just a novelty and that once the new wore off, tourists would return. These might have been some of the same people who said television would never replace radio.

In a desperate effort to stand their ground, the towns of Clanton, Thorsby, Jemison and Calera pooled their resources to erect billboards encouraging motorists to forsake I-65 and "Stay on 31." Using the time-honored designation as "Peach and Berry Center of Alabama," the colorful billboards promised "Good Food • Motels • Services • Water Sports." Tourists weren't paying attention and kept speeding down the interstate toward Mobile or Florida, leaving all those businesses to stare blankly at one another and wonder what had happened.

Go Jump in the Lake

One theme that resonates throughout history is that Alabama residents and tourists alike crave water activities. Maybe this is because of the state's predominantly rural background, with its "ol' swimmin' hole" tradition; maybe it has something to do with vacation season being the hottest of the summer months in the South, so trying to stay wet with something other than sweat was a major pursuit. There was the beach, of course, but that accounted for only a few miles along the very southern tip of Alabama. Scattered throughout the rest of the state were twenty-four (by one count) major natural lakes, but the ones that became the biggest tourist draws were the man-made variety. This really became a factor in the tourism industry in the early 1960s, but it was only the culmination of what had already been going on for about thirty years.

Near Alexander City, Alabama Power had begun buying up property around the Tallapoosa River in 1916, in preparation for constructing a dam and flooding the surroundings to create what would, at the time, be the largest man-made lake in the world: Lake Martin. (Its namesake? Alabama Power president Thomas M. Martin.) The dam and its resulting lake were dedicated in 1936.

Meanwhile, in the northern portion of Alabama, the Tennessee Valley Authority laid its plans to do much the same thing to the Tennessee River. The dam, creating the seventy-five-mile-long Lake Guntersville, was completed in 1939. Both Lake Martin and Lake Guntersville became major tourist centers in the post–World War II world. Lake Martin's Kowaliga Beach was popularized by Alabama native Hank Williams in his song "Kaw-

Liga," about a lovesick wooden Indian, of all things. No such carving existed at the time the song was such a hit, but after Williams's death in 1953, an appropriate Kaw-Liga statue was placed at the beach bearing its name. Not far away, Wind Creek Park offered one thousand acres of activities, including a white sand beach (always a popular concept for those who lived far from the Gulf), an observation tower, a gift shop, five hundred barbecue pits and picnic tables, a sightseeing boat tour and Sunday worship services held in a wooded glade. Lake Guntersville remained famous primarily for its fishing, although as we shall see, in the 1970s at least a few other activities came along to give tourists something else to do.

One thing all of the man-made lakes had in common was that they occupied land that had formerly been farms, highways and even entire towns. The residents, whether they wanted to leave or not, would be moved out so their ancestral homelands could be flooded, sometimes leaving melancholy relics that can still be seen on the lake bottoms.

That was certainly the case with a lake (and dam) that had its formal dedication in May 1961. Lewis M. Smith Dam (Smith was yet another former Alabama Company president), on the Sipsey Fork of the Warrior River, created Smith Lake out of the hills and ridges of Winston and Cullman Counties. At the time of its construction, Smith Lake was designated as forty-one miles long, but because its many branches flowed into valleys throughout the region, it had a total shoreline of more than five hundred miles.

Smith Lake itself was, and remains, its own attraction, although some hotels and small motels dot its shores for those who want something more luxurious (and air-conditioned) than a tent. There was more interest in commercial development in the eastern half of Alabama, where Lake Logan Martin splashed out of the Coosa River in 1964. Strategically, its shores began at Riverside, the spot where the always-under-construction I-20 crossed old U.S. 78. Much more than Smith Lake, Lake Logan Martin inspired dozens of marinas and related tourist businesses, including campgrounds, motels, restaurants, service stations and even the hallmark of a true tourist center, a Holiday Inn, which raised its giant flashing neon star in 1967.

An ad for the Nation's Innkeeper's grand opening at Riverside mentions such on-site amusements as golf, sailing, water skiing, gourmet smorgasbord dining, a white sand beach (natch), a swimming pool and an adjacent marina. Yes, whether one wanted to rough it or enjoy lakeside living in style, Alabama's man-made lakes were the places to do it.

For Whom the Bell Tolls

On Monday, October 16, 1961, newspapers carried the sad news of the passing of one of Alabama's true tourism pioneers:

> *Silence shrouds St. Bernard Abbey in Cullman today. Only the mournful hum of monks at their office and the deep, deliberate stroke of the death bell pierces the still air. It is a sound hushed, yet powerful; sorrowing, yet joyful. It is the requiem for a monk.*
>
> *The bell tolls for Brother Joseph Zoettl, creator of world-famous Ave Maria Grotto. The last remaining member of the German monks who established a Benedictine monastery in Cullman died in the abbey infirmary on Sunday.*

Not that Zoettl's departure from one world into the next was a surprise. His work in the tourist attraction he had inadvertently begun had slowed considerably once he reached his eightieth birthday in 1958. His final creations for the gardens were an American flag fashioned from glass pieces set in cement and a replica of the World's Peace Church, built on the site of the atomic bomb explosion in Hiroshima, Japan.

His health had begun to decline to a noticeable extent in the spring of 1961, even to the point of having his last rites performed, but defying all the odds he was up and about again until his death on October 15. He was buried in the abbey cemetery, with only a simple cross bearing his name to mark the spot—just as he would have wanted it, one suspects.

With Zoettl having moved on to the next life for which he had spent so many years in preparation, someone had to take over his job of maintaining the earthly creations he had begun. Leo Schwaiger Jr. began doing repair work on them in 1963, after the original Noah's Ark and Tower of Babel scenes were damaged by a tornado. In 1970, Schwaiger did what no other mortal had been able to accomplish, and that was to add new creations to the existing scenery. Appropriately, his first creation (following Zoettl's style) was a miniature of the abbey of St. Bernard itself. He continued to add new structures from time to time, as well as repairing and rebuilding the older ones, for most of the next twenty-five years.

Of all the many and varied tourist spots throughout Alabama, it is hard to think of another with a single founder and caretaker of Joseph Zoettl's influence, yet he preferred to remain anonymous. For that, he earned the respect of those of all different religions, who continue to visit his 1930s-era shrine to this day.

Rocks Around the Clock

In the previous chapter, we delved underground with the founders of Rickwood Caverns and Cathedral Caverns, and this chapter proves that caves and rocks were just as important in the 1960s as they had been a decade earlier. One characteristic they shared with those predecessors was that locals had known about them for generations, but it took some business-savvy entrepreneurs to pull them into the tourism-happy world of the 1960s.

Up on Chandler Mountain, in Blount County, there was a piece of property that bore a strong resemblance to the famed Rock City of Lookout Mountain. This acreage was known as Horse Pens 40, because one forty-acre section traditionally used some of the rock formations as a natural corral. The Hyatt family had homesteaded Horse Pens 40 (and other forty-acre tracts around it) since the early 1900s, but it was newspaper writer Warren Musgrove who stumbled across the rock-heavy rolling terrain in the 1950s while he was in the neighborhood to do a story about tomato farming. Finally, in 1961, he got some investors together and turned the stony acres into an attraction.

For decades, Horse Pens 40 was as well known for its folk music and handicrafts demonstrations as for its giant rocks. Those rocks, though, were never small pebbles in its publicity. Some of them bore an obvious resemblance to their name, such as Mushroom Rock, Shelter Rock and Elephant Rock, while others required a bit more imagination (Headless Hen Rock?). Horse Pens 40's postcards also had somewhat of a split personality. Many of them showed Native Americans in full regalia posing with the various sights, while others featured a cutoffs-clad blonde who looked like she might have leaped straight out of the *Li'l Abner* comic strip.

Horse Pens 40 benefited greatly by being only a short drive off busy U.S. 231, one of Alabama's busy north–south tourist routes. In fact, that highway came equipped with its own amenities meant for those who were on their way to somewhere else. For many years, a picnic area alongside 231 featured a replica Conestoga covered wagon on which kids could climb and have their photos taken. The wagon sat by the side of the road even after the picnic tables were long gone, slowly rotting away until only its wheels and axles were visible. Today, even those have disappeared back into the overgrowth. The city of Oneonta was another popular stop along U.S. 231, with a pair of restaurants that became legendary to travelers: the Around the Clock, with a large neon clock to illustrate its name, and Jonah's, which sat on a busy corner with an ersatz lighthouse on the roof and wooden cutout whales encircling the eaves.

Horse Pens 40 was an amazing collection of rock formations atop Chandler Mountain. For this publicity shot, "Chief" Henry Lambert (who billed himself as the "World's Most Photographed Indian") came down from his normal bailiwick in Cherokee, North Carolina, to lend a hand and a headdress.

Elephant Rock at Horse Pens 40 near Ashville, Ala.

When Horse Pens 40's postcards were not featuring Native Americans, they starred this unidentified blond model who greatly resembled Daisy Mae of the *Li'l Abner* comic strip.

Quite similar to Horse Pens 40 was Hurricane Creek Park, developed by William Rodgers next to U.S. 31, just north of Cullman. Its advertising took a somewhat different approach, characterizing it as "a trip into a Snuffy Smith Land of swinging bridges, hanging cliffs and ol' swimmin' hole." Those who responded to the ads did not see costumed comic strip hillbillies but a 175-foot-deep ravine with access provided by stairs fashioned from railroad crossties.

Around the same time Warren Musgrove was rounding up stray tourists to visit Horse Pens 40 and William Rodgers was making breezes with Hurricane Creek, over at Fort Payne, Myron Raymond was getting ready to introduce his own visitors to Manitou Cave. What's a Manitou? According to the linguists, that was the Cherokee word for "Great Spirit." Got that?

Manitou Cave had enjoyed its first burst of activity in the late 1880s, when pioneers held dances in a large, natural "ballroom" nestled among the subterranean formations. Those days were long over by the time Myron Raymond got hold of the property, and as one press release described it:

> *Modern man has waved his nuclear-age wand over the dark interior to convert it into an underground park. Stalactites and stalagmites gleam in their natural colors under 65,000 watts of indirect lighting. Steel bridges span a stream flowing at 300,000 gallons a day, the source of which has never been found.*

Part of that description was a pointed sneer at most cavern attractions that used colored lighting to make their formations seem more appealing; a handful, Manitou included, chose white light and let nature's colors do the rest. Of the many cave attractions that operated in Alabama over the years, Manitou Cave is one of the few that is no longer open to the public. At some point, it was closed as an attraction but is still made available to groups of spelunkers who wish to explore its depths at their own risk.

Two other cave attractions from the same period of tourism—and perhaps prehistory, too—were Russell Cave and Guntersville Caverns. Russell Cave was not as much a commercial attraction, since it had been declared a National Monument in 1961. Archaeological digs similar to what had long gone on in Moundville were the main activity at Russell Cave, although the traces of civilization this work uncovered dated back much further than those—6,500 years, according to some estimates.

Guntersville Caverns was a more typical commercial cave, with the usual approach of finding some unique feature to promote. In this case, it was the

Manitou Cave, near Fort Payne, joined the rest of Alabama's underground attractions in the early 1960s. Its souvenir plate depicted colorful scenes of its subterranean sights.

"Whosababies." Whosa-*what*-now, you say? This was the nickname given to the small calcite formations that resembled elves. This cavern was also quite proud of its natural rock rendition of Mary, Joseph and baby Jesus, sculpted by nature rather than Joseph Zoettl.

Yet another rocky collection could be found at the appropriately named Bama Rock Gardens near Vance. Once described as being how Rock City would have appeared had it been located in Cherokee, North Carolina, the Bama Rock Gardens had a similar collection of erosion-created rock formations, all intertwined with the history of the Creek tribe that once called it home. Bama Rock Gardens Road still appears on today's maps, but like Manitou Cave, it is now closed to the public and available only to those adventurous souls who want to use its cliffs and bluffs for hiking and exploring.

Liberty Belles, Baboons and Bananas

Tourists looking for something to do in downtown Birmingham after having visited Vulcan Park had a new choice as of the end of May 1962. For years, the home office of Liberty National Insurance had advertised its presence with a neon rendition of the company logo atop its ten-story building. In the early 1960s, Liberty National decided to take the logical next step and replaced the neon logo with an actual thirty-one-foot-tall replica of the Statue of Liberty, proudly perched on a prodigious pedestal overlooking Twentieth Street.

Not content with winning a Freedom Foundation award for its Liberty replica, on May 31, 1962, the insurance company inaugurated its "Miss Liberty Tour." Two separate observation platforms were connected by the Tip of the Torch Room, where photographs were displayed showing the construction of the twenty-thousand-pound figure, as well as slides promoting other attractions in the Greater Birmingham area. The forty-minute tours were conducted by "personable, attractive and patriotically attired young ladies" known as, what else, Liberty Belles.

The Miss Liberty Tour qualifies as an attraction that will never be seen again in Alabama. In 1989, the miniature Liberty was moved from its lofty downtown perch to the new office complex in the suburbs known as Liberty Park. It can still be seen there to this day, but its former pedestal sits abandoned and empty on the old site, looking a bit lonely without Liberty.

One of the other Birmingham attractions visitors to the Tip of the Torch Room would have seen promoted was the city zoo, which for several years had been developing from a local novelty to a park famed throughout Alabama. Named after the Birmingham mayor who was one of its biggest boosters, the Jimmy Morgan Zoo had begun in 1955 with a single exhibit, Monkey Island, a moat-surrounded rock pile inhabited by dozens of comical spider monkeys. The site chosen for the zoo had formerly been a fish hatchery, and the up-and-coming park benefited from the abundance of WPA-era rockwork already situated throughout the property.

As the 1950s gave way to the 1960s, the Jimmy Morgan Zoo continued to expand, adding more and more varieties of animals in assorted habitats. There was even an indoor room known as the Rainforest, which simulated the look and feel of a tropical jungle and provided a suitable residence for tropical birds and reptiles. A miniature train chugged around the property, at one point passing the mock grave of the legendary Casey Jones, whose boots sticking up out of the dirt were the only evidence of his earthly

IN BIRMINGHAM
it's the
"MISS LIBERTY" TOUR

LIBERTY NATIONAL'S AWARD WINNING STATUE OF LIBERTY
Atop The Home Office Building At 301 South 20th St.

When the Liberty National Insurance Company installed this scaled-down replica of the famous statue on its downtown Birmingham office building, it was only natural that it make it the climax of a tour that also helped promote other local attractions.

The Birmingham Botanical Gardens opened in December 1962. The conservatory, with fountain and floral clock outside and banana trees bearing fruit inside, was the centerpiece of the horticultural display.

existence. Separated from the main part of the zoo by the parking lot, the Children's Zoo gave kids a chance for some face-to-face time with smaller, cuddlier creatures.

The neighborhood where the Jimmy Morgan Zoo sat was known as Lane Park, and in 1962, the four-footed residents got a new neighbor. There had been a drive to establish a botanical garden across the street, and in December 1962 the new Birmingham Botanical Gardens conservatory had its grand opening. The gigantic greenhouse was set up as a sort of indoor park of its own, with a full-size gristmill and water wheel in one corner. One of the initial sights once inside the door was a huge banana tree, giving thousands of Alabama kids their first—and for some, only—glimpse of how bananas looked on the stalk instead of in the produce department.

While the conservatory was the centerpiece of the gardens, the most visible trademark of the new attraction was a twenty-six-foot-wide floral clock donated by Mrs. Horace Hammond. It was dedicated on the gentle

This authentic teahouse was added to Birmingham's Japanese Gardens in 1967. It had formerly served as part of Japan's exhibit at the 1964–65 New York World's Fair.

slope in front of the conservatory just in time for spring 1963. The clock's face was composed of five thousand flowers, with a twelve-foot-long minute hand. The floral clock remained the emblem of the Birmingham Botanical Gardens until 1995, when it was removed because of its deteriorating interior works. Today, its spot is occupied by a concrete and bronze sculpture that vaguely resembles a clock, as a sort of memorial.

Soon after the gardens opened, plans were drawn up for an important addition to be known as the Japanese Gardens. Just as the conservatory and floral clock were centerpieces of the main gardens, the Japanese Gardens would have their own symbol: an authentic Japanese teahouse that had been part of that country's pavilion at the 1964–65 New York World's Fair. The Japanese Trade Association readily agreed to donate its exhibit to Birmingham; getting the teahouse from the fairgrounds to Alabama required a bit of international intrigue, however.

In November 1965, worker Fritz Woehle told the *Birmingham News* how this feat was accomplished:

> *We found mass confusion around the teahouse site. Since Japan had not paid taxes on sales during the Fair, the government had closed off the area*

and was breaking up everything. The truck driver and I quickly took down whole teahouse walls at one time. Since there were no nails, we could pull the pegs out of intricate parts. We did this disassembling in less than a day and went out the way we entered. In reassembling it, we had only our pictures, but it worked out fine.

Skullduggery notwithstanding, Birmingham's Japanese Gardens were dedicated in May 1967, with the rescued teahouse serving as the site of an official tea ceremony with the Japanese ambassador.

THE SHIP OF STATE

Ironically, while the City of Birmingham was laying its plans for the Japanese Gardens, at the other end of the state there was a flurry of activity concerning one of the warships that had made it possible to defeat Japan twenty years before. It had all begun a few years earlier, in the summer of 1962, when word got out that the U.S. Navy was about to scrap the 1942 battleship that had been christened the USS *Alabama*. After seeing action in both the Atlantic and Pacific during World War II, the *Alabama* had been decommissioned in 1947 and placed in storage at the navy facility in Bremerton, Washington.

With the news that the *Alabama* was about to become thirty-five thousand tons of scrap metal, the state for which the vessel was named sprang into action. Politicians and citizens alike helped formulate the idea that the *Alabama* should be displayed at a newly created park at Mobile Bay, as a shrine to the state's human contribution to multiple wars. (There was probably some inspiration by a similar move the previous year, when the citizens of North Carolina undertook the task of rescuing their own named vessel, the USS *North Carolina*, from a similar fate and made it into an attraction at Wilmington.)

Relocating the *Alabama* involved towing the ship 5,600 miles from Seattle, through the Panama Canal and up to Mobile, for which Alabamians raised a reported $1 million. The authorities were particularly proud of Alabama's schoolkids, who donated nearly $100,000 in nickels, dimes and quarters.

The new Battleship Memorial Park, to use its formal name, was dedicated on January 9, 1965. Naturally, a tour of the centerpiece ship was the main feature, and since it would have been contrary to the park's purposes to

The World War II battleship USS *Alabama* was scheduled to become scrap metal, but a fundraising drive by the citizens of the state resulted in its becoming the lynchpin of Battleship Memorial Park in Mobile in 1965.

fundamentally alter the Alabama, little was done to make it any easier for landlubbers to crawl about its decks. Colored arrows helped guide visitors along, but a complete tour still required some climbing of ladders and otherwise getting about just as Popeye's contemporaries would have done. The official guide brochure made this perfectly clear:

> For an orderly and complete tour of the ship it is suggested you follow the numbered arrows. Near these arrows you will find plaques describing the ship's features and equipment. Visitors are cautioned that the construction of a battleship offers many hazards to the unwary, such as low doorways, high doorsills, and fittings and obstruction about the deck. PLEASE BE CAREFUL!

A few years after its opening, Battleship Memorial Park gained a co-star for the USS *Alabama*, the retired submarine USS *Drum*. Placed in the water behind the *Alabama* (but thankfully not fully submerged), the *Drum* gave visitors a taste of the other form of World War II water warfare. By the late 1990s, there was a movement to take the *Drum* out of the drink and display it on dry land, as its relatively minuscule size was continually causing it to be ignored by tourists in favor of the overwhelmingly bulky *Alabama*. (For comparison, the *Alabama* was 680 feet long and the shrimpy *Drum* only 311 feet long.)

Perhaps the most ironic event in the *Alabama*'s long history was its featured role in the 1987 made-for-TV movie *War and Remembrance*, based on the novel by Herman Wouk. The irony was not so much that the *Alabama* was cast as five different warships over the course of the film but that two of them were as enemy Japanese vessels. The *Alabama* rose to the occasion, however, and proved that it could play a villain as well as a hero.

As with most attractions that drew the attention (and crowds) that Battleship Memorial Park did, there were other businesses that glommed onto the periphery. One of the most promoted non-warship sights on Battleship Parkway was the Alabama Historama, which deserves some sort of credit for coming up with such a catchy name. Inside, the Historama was one of those miniature relief maps so popular at other attractions (Chattanooga's Confederama comes to mind), where tabletop history ("from the arrival of Hernando de Soto to the Space Age") was played out repeatedly all day long for curious tourists.

THE ROAD THROUGH THE FOREST

Perhaps the most unlikely place to find a tourist attraction of any sort was alongside State Highway 33 as it cut a gentle path through the Bankhead National Forest. Before peeling back the foliage to take a look at that, though, perhaps a word or two about the Bankhead Forest is in order.

Taking in more than 181,000 acres and covering parts of Lawrence, Winston and Franklin Counties, the national forest was first set aside in 1918 and named the Alabama National Forest; in 1936, it was renamed the Black Warrior National Forest and got its permanent Bankhead appellation in 1942. In case you are wondering, it was not named after the same Bankhead as the highway (John), but rather his son (William), who was also a longtime U.S. representative. William was also the father of legendary actress Tallulah Bankhead, who was already a star by the time the tree tract was named in her dad's honor.

See Alabama First

In the middle of the Bankhead National Forest, a re-creation of a typical pioneer homestead greeted those who were traveling through the woods. It even featured a replica moonshine still with attendant hillbillies.

As with most "all-natural" areas, the main tourist activities in the Bankhead Forest were camping and fishing. In the spring of 1963, a pharmacist from Moulton, Hudson Sandlin, decided to do a little something more. He established what was widely promoted as the "Pioneer Homestead" in the community of Hepsidam. Now, don't bother trying to find that town name on your Alabama road map; it isn't there, and when it did exist, Sandlin's pioneer attraction and a store were the only things in it. In fact, it is impossible to determine just where this five-acre tourist stop was, as the forest has reclaimed its site.

While it existed, the Pioneer Homestead was popular enough to be listed in all state tourism literature. One reason for its popularity is that it was totally free; the only charge was for items in the neighboring store. F.E. Armstrong, the storekeeper, told a reporter that at times the Pioneer Homestead had welcomed up to five hundred visitors in one day. And what did those visitors see? A log cabin containing the everyday household items that would have been used in that part of the state a century before, and outdoors, a replica moonshine still complete with costumed hillbillies. The log cabin was actually built from four such

Joseph Zoettl was the creative genius behind Cullman's Ave Maria Grotto on the grounds of St. Bernard's Abbey. The diminutive Benedictine monk humbly posed for this handsome portrait in front of some of his miniature creations.

VISIT BELLINGRATH Gardens

CHARM SPOT of the DEEP SOUTH

NEAR MOBILE, ALABAMA

US 90

Bellingrath Gardens was famous for its annual springtime display of azaleas, so it was natural that the cover shot for this brochure was made while those flowers were at the height of their splendor.

It could easily be argued that the mounds at Moundville hardly qualified as prehistoric, since they dated from the 1500s, but billboards such as these no doubt got many traveling families to pull off the highway to see what all the fuss was about.

The chain of Wigwam Village tourist courts was based in Cave City, Kentucky. Alabama's only example was on U.S. 11, between Birmingham and Bessemer, and opened in 1940. No trace of the concrete tepees exists on the spot today. *Warren Nelson collection.*

Saxon's was a chain of candy and souvenir stores based near Anniston. After restaurants were added to the format in the 1950s, Saxon's became a welcome stop for travelers throughout Alabama and into neighboring states as well.

Alabama took a cue from the other successful tourism-heavy states and relied as much as possible on attractive ladies to help sell itself as a vacation destination.

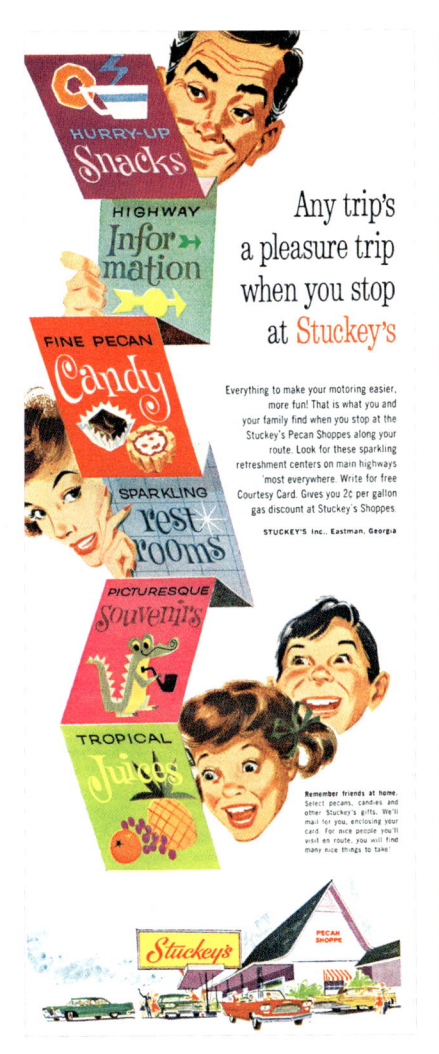

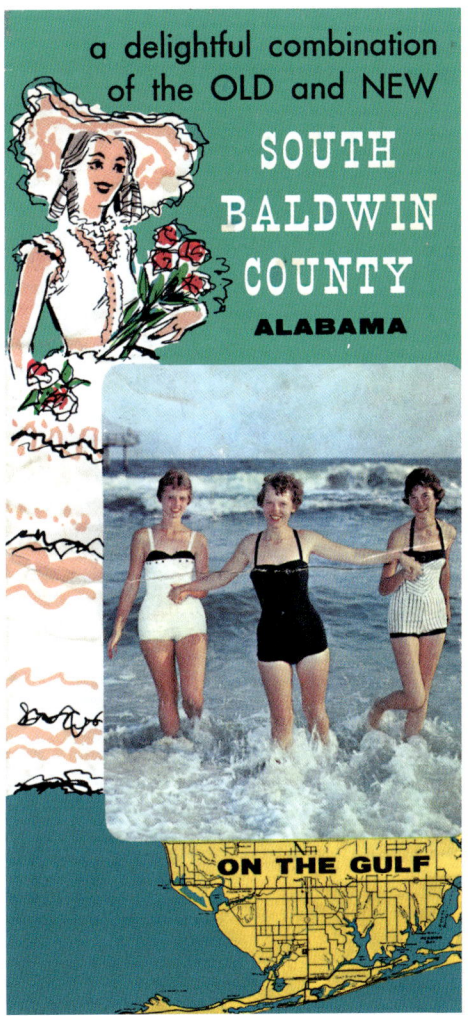

Above left: Stuckey's came to Alabama in the 1950s with a handful of locations along the old federal highways. Once the interstate system began creeping across the state, Stuckey's became a pioneer at establishing outposts at exits where there was no other commercial business.

Above right: At the time of this brochure, the beaches of Baldwin County—namely Gulf Shores and Orange Beach—were just beginning their commercial development to lure vacationers from the Florida Panhandle to the immediate east.

Above: After Rickwood Caverns left the world of commercial attractions and became a state park, its traditional red-and-white billboards were phased out. This lone example, forgotten and partly hidden by foliage, was still standing along U.S. 31 in Fultondale in 1996.

Left: Cathedral Caverns was proud of "Goliath," recognized as the world's largest stalagmite. This postcard used normal-sized human beings to give an ample idea of Goliath's girth.

When Alabama's first Holiday Inn opened on U.S. 11 near Bessemer in 1954, the chain was so new that the iconic "Great Sign" had to include the word "Hotel" for those who had never heard of a Holiday Inn. *Dixie Neon collection.*

Hank Williams composed his song "Kaw-Liga," about a lovesick wooden Indian, in a cabin on Lake Martin. After Williams's death, this tribute to his work was erected at Kowaliga Beach.

A focal point of Birmingham's Botanical Gardens, opened in 1962, was this floral clock that kept accurate time via an underground mechanism. The working clock was later replaced by a sculpture that represented a clock without having to actually work.

The World War II battleship USS *Alabama* was rescued from the impending scrap heap and towed to Mobile to become an attraction in 1965. This stunning aerial view gives some idea of the scope of Battleship Memorial Park.

Left: It would appear that Daisy Mae had leaped from the panels of the *Li'l Abner* comic strip to take on extra work promoting Horse Pens 40, a collection of eccentric rock formations atop Chandler Mountain.

Below: No, it isn't Florida's Six Gun Territory or North Carolina's Ghost Town in the Sky. It's Gardendale's Dry Gulch Ghost Town on U.S. 31, an adjunct to that city's Grub Stake Restaurant in the 1960s.

By the 1970s, Gulf Shores had come into its own and offered a variety of attractions that aped Florida's Miracle Strip in a more low-budget sort of way. In the lower left-hand corner, notice the small, unnamed amusement park and miniature golf course. *J.D. Weeks collection.*

The Sunnyland Cottages, with their coating of neon-blue paint, were typical examples of the small cinder-block motels that lined Gulf Shores and Orange Beach up until September 1979, when Hurricane Frederic turned the Alabama coast into one big blank slate.

CANYON LAND PARK

Near Fort Payne, Alabama

CHAIRLIFT INTO THE DEEPEST GORGE EAST OF THE MISSISSIPPI RIVER

- HORSEBACK RIDING
- ENTERTAINMENT
- PICNICKING
- SWIMMING
- FUN RIDES
- CAMPING
- FISHING
- HIKING
- ZOO

CANYON LAND–AN EXCITING WORLD

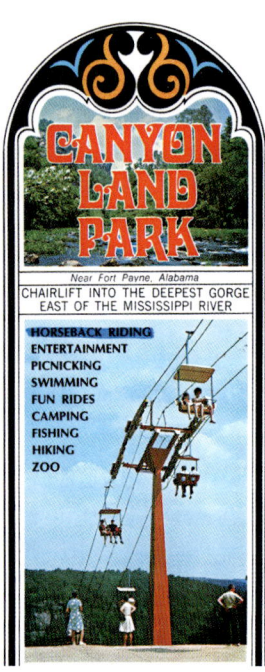

In the heart of DeSoto State Park, featuring famous DeSoto Falls, Canyon Land Park takes you back-to-nature with a quiet excitement. Refresh yourself with a free swim in the sparkling waters of Little River — one of only three unpolluted rivers left in the United States today. Fish or picnic. Plan an outing for your school, club, church or where you work and take advantage of reduced rates on various amusements for large groups.

Hear the nation's top recording stars in person like you've never heard them before! Free for the listening each Saturday evening and night on Canyon Land's giant stage. (For the free shows, just take the Chairlift.)

IT'S FUN-TASTIC ❧ 200 CAMPSITES ❧ FUN RIDES

Opposite, top: Fort Payne's Canyon Land Park remains a hazy memory for hundreds of Alabama vacationers. During its brief life, it featured a zoo, a train ride, vintage amusement rides and a chairlift down into the gorge of Little River Canyon.

Opposite, bottom: Travelers throughout northern Alabama were bombarded by these painted signs for the Western Auto store in Dora, even though it was not a tourist attraction. This was the last-known example of the dozens of signs and was photographed on the Walker/Cullman County line in 2005.

Above: Take some time (and a magnifying glass) and try to imagine what an impact there would have been if this grand plan for a Space City, USA theme park near Huntsville had actually been built. The project began with much fanfare in 1964, but by three years later what few park features had been completed were auctioned off and the property left abandoned. *Lance George collection.*

Decatur's Point Mallard Park became a tourist destination with its wave pool that simulated swimming in the ocean. Many future water parks in Alabama would follow Point Mallard's lead.

Another shoot-'em-up Wild West town in Alabama was Legiontown, USA, on U.S. 11 near Ashville. When the cowboys were not shooting it out in the street, visitors could tour a museum devoted to the career of legendary TV personality Country Boy Eddy.

Above: Birmingham's Sloss Furnaces became an outdoor museum of the iron and steel industry in 1983. This postcard depicted Sloss during its more active days, before it ceased operations in 1970.

Left: The outdoor emblem of the Red Mountain Museum was Seymour, a fiberglass brontosaurus formerly employed at a Sinclair service station. When the museum merged with the nearby Discovery Place to become the McWane Science Center, Seymour's carcass was left behind to be ravaged by vandals.

Decals were an important part of any vacation trip, and these six are only a few of the many designs that promoted Alabama over the decades. *Sjef Van Eijk collection*.

cabins, moved from their original locations and connected together to make a single museum.

There are no records to confirm just how long the Pioneer Homestead, or the community of Hepsidam, existed or the eventual fate of the log cabin and its contents. All that can be certain is that, of all the attractions that have ever dotted the Alabama highways, it was the most major one to be totally forgotten and blotted out of tourists' memories today.

From Barn Roofs to Underground

One might think that by the 1960s, every eligible cave in the state had already been developed for its tourist potential—but one would be wrong. Among the few that were still sitting in their natural condition was one near Valley Head, just off U.S. 11, that had been known as Ellis Cave since the 1890s. As with so many other future attractions we have seen, Ellis Cave had been a source of pride for its owners (the Ellis family, naturally) for decades; they had documented carvings and inscriptions dating back to 1824, and the cave had been a popular gathering spot since the dawn of the twentieth century. However, no tourist literature mentioned Ellis Cave, and it never would—at least under that name.

At some point around 1964, the cave was leased from the Ellis family by a pair of developers, Alva Hammond and Clark Byers, who saw its potential for attracting tourists on then-busy U.S. 11. Not much is known about Hammond, but Byers certainly knew his way around the tourism business. Since 1935, he had been gainfully employed by Rock City Gardens, about thirty-five miles north, to paint variations of its famed SEE ROCK CITY slogan on barn roofs from Michigan to the Florida state line. Byers obviously picked up an idea or two about how to operate a successful roadside attraction because most of the way he approached his new acquisition was directly related to how he had promoted Rock City for the previous thirty years.

First, knowing that the name Ellis Cave was not going to mean anything except to locals, Byers renamed the site Sequoyah Caverns, after the famed Cherokee scholar who invented an alphabet for his nation. (Although to date no one has come up with any hard evidence to prove that Sequoyah was one of the early tourists to visit the cave that would later be named for him, it is true that for a number of years he lived in a Cherokee village just south

Sequoyah Caverns covered northeastern Alabama with painted barn roofs such as this one. And why not? One of the caverns' developers was Clark Byers, who had painted the SEE ROCK CITY barn roofs since 1935. Notice at right a smaller piggybacked sign for nearby Manitou Cave.

of the property.) Every cave needed some sort of feature to separate it from the rest, and Byers seized on Sequoyah Caverns's "looking glass lakes," the subterranean pools that reflected the stalactites and other formations once they were properly lighted.

Byers applied his long-honed talent for sign painting to promoting his new attraction. Barns and billboards that were not already being used by Rock City became his canvases for Sequoyah Caverns. In some cases, Byers was able to make good use of a single structure, with one side of a barn advertising Sequoyah and the other side carrying a Rock City message, depending on the north–south flow of traffic. He also gave his longtime employer an oblique

After Clark Byers suffered an accident while on the job, Rock City purchased the controlling interest in Sequoyah Caverns. As seen here, billboards for both attractions frequently appeared side-by-side along the highways.

nod with the slogan he used for Sequoyah Caverns. Since Rock City's barn roofs and billboards dubbed the mountaintop attraction the "World's Eighth Wonder," Byers loyally referred to his own park as "World's Ninth Wonder." Since 1939, Rock City had been charming tourists with its herd of white fallow deer, and Byers exported a few of those to Sequoyah Caverns, where their descendants contentedly graze away to this day.

Byers had done a lot of work in getting Sequoyah Caverns ready for the public, but his association with the new attraction was unfortunately cut short. In 1968, while repainting a Rock City billboard near Murfreesboro, Tennessee, Byers was electrocuted by some low-hanging power lines blown against the metal sign by a passing truck. Although he later recovered with no appreciable side effects, in the short term he was no longer able to work and keep up the lease payments on Sequoyah Caverns. Rock City repaid Byers's decades of loyalty by assuming the lease in his stead, taking over the operation in late March 1969. Byers, during his recuperation, remained on the new Sequoyah Caverns Corporation board of directors.

To handle Sequoyah Caverns' business dealings, Rock City assigned its own advertising manager, Dick Borden, who (like Byers) had spent most of his previous career on the road. Rather than painting signs, it had been Borden's responsibility to see that Rock City's advertising appeared in every motel, restaurant and service station in the Southeast, and now he was going to get to stay home for a while and get Sequoyah Caverns back on track.

Soon after Borden took the reins, Sequoyah became the fourth Alabama facility in the KOA (Kampgrounds of America) chain. Newspapers announced that the standard A-frame headquarters building, emblematic of the KOA chain, would house a self-service laundry, restrooms with hot showers and a camp store. Under Rock City's ownership and management, improvements at Sequoyah Caverns proceeded apace, and well into the 1980s the number of its billboards (and, still, an occasional barn) were rivaled only by Rock City's along the I-59 corridor between Gadsden and Chattanooga.

The State's Most Spaced-Out City

If Sequoyah Caverns was one of the most-advertised attractions in the state, and the Pioneer Homestead in the Bankhead Forest was one of the most-promoted attractions to disappear without a trace, there is only one viable candidate for the most-advertised, most-promoted attraction that never actually existed. That would be the famous theme park Space City, USA. You remember hearing about it, don't you? Near Huntsville? Built on the Disneyland model? The first theme park in the Southeast? No? Nothing, huh?

Well, to figure out just what happened, we have to begin in January 1964, when a press conference was held in Huntsville to unveil plans for the two-hundred-acre amusement park, complete with impressive artistic renderings of how some of its features would look. Generally speaking, Space City, USA, was to be laid out in a fashion similar to Disneyland in California—the inspiration for all theme parks that followed its 1955 opening, it seems—in that visitors would enter through a main plaza and then branch off from a "hub" into the various themed sections. The unique selling point for Space City, USA, is that the "hub" would represent a time machine that transported its guests to the various past and future eras depicted in the rest of the park.

Just what were those other sections? you ask, barely able to contain your enthusiasm. One was the Lost World, a prehistoric land with dinosaurs and

The Story of Alabama Tourism

SPACE CITY USA agrees with the authorities!
The planned rides at Space City now number 23. These include: the Caveman Ride, Dinosaur Dark Ride, Stern Wheeler Boat Ride, Antique Car Ride, Flying Saucer Ride, Space Platform Ride, Jet Car Ride, Carousel, and Jack and the Beanstalk Slide. The total rides planned will accommodate over 14,000 people per hour.

If all the plans for a huge theme park known as Space City, USA, had actually come to pass, Huntsville would have had an attraction to rival the forthcoming Six Flags Over Georgia, Opryland and Walt Disney World. Unfortunately, Space City, USA, never even got off its launching pad.

a belching volcano; adjoining that would be the Old South, with magnolias, mint juleps and showboats. Moon City would represent the future, and Old Travel Town was only vaguely defined. The Land of Oz apparently bore no relationship to L. Frank Baum's classic story but was the area for standard kiddie rides. Out on the lake that was a major part of the scenery would have been Dead Man's Island, with a pirate theme (you were expecting maybe Easter bunnies?). Of course, all the usual theme park elements from a train ride to indoor dark rides to a skyride from one side of the park to the other were part of the plan.

All of this was to have been located along State Highway 20, south of what is now I-565. The team charged with bringing the project from paper to reality boasted that in addition to Disneyland, it had been involved in the creation of Six Flags Over Texas, Pleasure Island (Boston, Massachusetts), Legend City (Phoenix, Arizona) and Freedomland (Bronx Borough, New York). What was not stated was that other than Walt's world and the original Six Flags near Dallas, all of the other parks had been financial disasters, and some were already on the verge of shutting down permanently. Perhaps Huntsville just got lucky.

The company sold stock in Space City, USA, and managed to raise enough money for initial construction. Most people are surprised to learn that anything at all got built on the site, but fading newspaper photos confirm that at least the volcano, the railroad station in the Old South section, a dark ride building and a few fanciful structures for the Land of Oz did exist once. During all the hoopla of the first announcement, an opening date of 1965 was scheduled. When 1965 arrived and there was still nothing to see, the projected grand opening was pushed further and further into the future. By September 1967, Huntsville seemed resigned to the fact that it was never going to happen. A newspaper article ominously headlined "Costly Park Lies in Decay" described the site as overgrown with foliage and the few completed structures rusting away. Those remnants were auctioned off in October 1967, at least ensuring they would have a life at other amusement parks throughout the country. For example, the train ride is said to still be in operation in Santa Margarita, California.

After sitting dormant for decades, the property that was to have been Space City, USA, was redeveloped into an upscale neighborhood known as Edgewater. The lake is still there, and while the residential area was being constructed, workers found abandoned concrete slabs and an occasional outbuilding left over from the failed theme park project. What was to have been the concrete path for the "Cave Man Car Ride" in the Lost World still exists near the Edgewater clubhouse. Otherwise, Space City, USA, has been as forgotten as if it never existed—and it didn't.

Deep in the Heart of Dixie

Most successful theme parks attract ancillary business around them, all hoping to get in on some of those flowing tourist dollars. The streets around Disneyland became so choked with motels, restaurants and competing attractions that good old Uncle Walt determined he was not going to make the same mistake when he began buying vast acreage of swampland in central Florida. However, Space City, USA, had not even gotten off its launching pad yet when another attraction began making plans to enter its orbit.

A Huntsville company called TEC Productions pitched plans for a miniature park to be known as Alabama Showcase, squeezing the entire outline of the state into a one-acre tract. The prospectus gave an idea of just how optimistic the plans were:

> *The overall concept is a miniature topographical model of the state, with emphasis on waterways, natural resources, industry, tourist attractions and other available facilities. Participating groups will be responsible for their respective portions of the showcase; however, control specifications will be provided to insure a well-coordinated presentation.*
>
> *The Alabama Showcase should be located in an area where a maximum number of people can view it and benefit from the experience. Space City USA, a major theme park being developed in Madison, is proposed as the most desirable location for this project. It is estimated that over one million people per year will visit Space City USA, which will cover approximately 60 acres and will be similar to the world-famous Disneyland. The planned opening for this project is April 1965.*

Well, as Space City, USA, went, so went the Alabama Showcase. Even if the larger of the two parks had opened, the Alabama Showcase proposal sounds like it was relying awfully heavily on free donations from the various cities and industries to be represented in it. The idea of building it in the shape of the state sounds like someone had been paying attention to the huge Freedomland theme park that opened in New York's Bronx in 1960, which took the shape of a map of the United States.

Considering that that enterprise survived for only four years, it should be obvious that Alabama hardly had a corner on failed attractions. With Space City a part of the not even distantly remembered past, memories of Alabama Showcase have been even more lost in the deepest recesses of the universe.

You Mean It Ain't Finished Yet?

With all the new existing and planned attractions competing for tourist dollars, it would seem that Alabama's interstate highway construction must have been nearing completion—right? Wrong. A 1961 newspaper headline had admiringly referred to the new system as making "fairy tale progress." Barely a year later, it was beginning to look like the only fairy tale characters to which it bore any resemblance were the tortoise and the hare…and it wasn't the long-eared one of those.

As we saw earlier, interstate construction tended to move most quickly in the areas between cities, where there was plenty of open countryside. The snag was generally when approaching suburban areas, when suddenly existing development (including entire neighborhoods) was in the way. Nowhere was this most evident than in Jefferson County, through which most tourist traffic passed no matter in which direction it was headed. In October 1962, officials alarmingly calculated that with the amount of work remaining to be done, at its present rate it would be nearly one hundred years before the planned interstate system in Jefferson County alone would be finished. Four years later, another survey showed that of the projected 130 miles of interstates in Birmingham and Jefferson County, 14 miles had been completed and another 13 were under construction. Even with those discouraging figures, the state highway department forged ahead with its announcement of yet another future interstate in the area, I-459, which would cut a semicircular loop south of Birmingham to help bypass traffic around the already congested city center. I-459 would be the first part of a projected loop, or beltline, that would encircle Birmingham.

(In case you would like to know, it was well into the 1980s before I-459 would be anything close to being finished. More than a dozen years into the twenty-first century, the northern half of the beltline would still exist only as tentative dotted lines on maps, with a hoped completion date decades into the future.)

The Story of Alabama Tourism

If you can figure out the meaning of this postcard, you're doing better than the rest of us. The caption on the back reads, "Try something BIG! Vacation in Beautiful Alabama! Perched precariously on a placid, but pompous pachyderm, children appear more solicitous than Shirley." It goes on to enumerate some of the attractions where live animals could be viewed, including the Jimmy Morgan Zoo, Sequoyah Caverns and Canyon Land Park, but never explains who Shirley is. Maybe she is the mini-skirted Native American princess?

One of the areas the beltline, had it existed, would have made it possible for travelers and residents alike to avoid was the spot near downtown Birmingham where I-65 and I-59 (and I-20, which at that point followed the same path as I-59) crossed each other. It is an ironic fact of tourism history that, in the days of the old federal highways, the spot where two of them intersected was generally the epitome of commercial and economic development, bringing in drivers from all directions. For the interstates, which were planned to be so much safer, the crossing of two or more of them generally produced only a driver's headache, especially if a transfer from one to another was needed.

So it was in Birmingham. In November 1966, initial work began on the huge I-65/I-59 interchange. It would be years before it was completed, but as anyone who has driven that route knows, it quickly earned its nickname "Malfunction Junction." Confusing and frequently inadequate merging lanes, added to the amount of traffic flowing through the intersection, made it an exciting adventure to navigate—and not the *good* type of exciting adventure. Ever since, Alabama's highway planners have pointed to Malfunction Junction as the textbook example of how *not* to build an interstate interchange, proving that even botched plans can have their advantages if used to prevent history from repeating itself.

Drive Slow and See Our Town; Drive Fast and See Our Jail

Just north of what would eventually be Malfunction Junction was the town of Gardendale, and since I-65 had not yet progressed to the point of bypassing the community, tourism was still based on U.S. 31 in that area. In July 1967, the Gardendale police force began using that newfangled radar stuff to enforce the speed limit on the busy north–south route. Almost immediately, just as in Harpersville back in the early 1950s, the Alabama Motorists Association jumped into the picture to claim that Gardendale was operating a speed trap.

As usual, each side had its own reasons for believing its case was the truthful one. For its side, Gardendale brought out some statistics that, pertinent to our discussion here, showed that traffic was actually increasing in that part of U.S. 31, even while it was declining in the counties north of Montgomery where I-65 had been completed. According to Gardendale's figures, during July 1967 there had been twenty-six wrecks, with seven fatalities, within its jurisdiction. For July 1966, there had been only six wrecks, and the alarming jump is what had prompted the installation of radar equipment. Of course, catching more speeders meant there were more disgruntled travelers to complain to the Alabama Motorists Association, and suddenly here we are back where this story began.

While the AMA and the police force were duking it out at city hall, another tourist-oriented business came to Gardendale. Anyone who did much vacation traveling during the 1960s knows that one genre of attraction that could be found from coast to coast was the western theme park. Florida had them; New York had them; even states in the real West had them. Alabama did not have one—yet. But in the late 1960s, just north of Gardendale on U.S. 31, Dry Gulch Ghost Town came a-moseyin' into the area.

Actually, Dry Gulch Ghost Town was merely an addition to the Grub Stake Restaurant, which decided to go whole hog by pigging out on its western theme. Local resident Wally Moseley had been collecting western

The Grub Stake Restaurant on U.S. 31 at Gardendale supplemented its dining room with an entire Dry Gulch Ghost Town, where cowboys and western hombres entertained. The complex burned in a spectacular fire in 1970, and today an antique store sits on its former concrete floor slab.

memorabilia for years, and it found its final resting place in the décor of the Grub Stake. As one of its postcards described the setting:

> *Grub Stake Restaurant in Dry Gulch Ghost Town is a living reminder of the old West. Tools, utensils, implements and weapons used by pioneers are on display, and also original paintings of many of the characters of renown of the 1870s and 1880s.*

Exterior views show the part of the restaurant that fronted on U.S. 31 to resemble a row of typical western buildings, while behind that was another row of buildings decorated as a saloon, the marshal's office and other sights one would expect to see in such a place. It also appears that cowboys on horseback roamed the parking lot to interact with those waiting to get inside.

Unfortunately, the Dry Gulch Ghost Town turned out to be a little too dry. One night in either 1969 or 1970 (accounts vary), the entire complex burned to the ground, including the priceless Moseley collection of artifacts. Almost immediately after the rubble was carted off to Boot Hill, an antique store was constructed using the same concrete floor slab, and it has remained in business ever since. The marshal, cowboys and horses are gone, but the Old West lives on at the site in the form of knickknacks available as antiques and collectibles. Dry Gulch would not be the last western town to be seen in Alabama, so don't put your spurs away yet. The next one may be a-waitin' just over the next ridge, podner.

Stuckey's Gets Stuck; Saxon's Gets Sacked

As the interstate highways crept across the Alabama landscape, one business that kept pace with them was Stuckey's. You will recall that when we last stopped in for a pecan log and rubber alligator, Stuckey's was still depending on the old U.S. highways for its Alabama locations. However, its biggest fame would come when the company became a pioneer in constructing its candy/souvenir stores at interstate exits in some of the most forlorn stretches. Today, it is hard to remember when there was not a service station or McDonald's at every exit; in the 1960s, frequently a Stuckey's was the only such facility encountered in miles and miles of interstate driving. Stuckey family legend has it that founder W.S. Stuckey had his own method for determining where a store was needed. They claim that W.S. would set out from a designated point—say, Atlanta or Nashville or Birmingham—and drive until he felt the need to visit a restroom. He figured that if it worked for him, there would undoubtedly be other travelers in the same predicament, so he would start looking for a piece of property.

In December 1964, the entire Stuckey's chain was sold to become a subsidiary of the Pet Milk Company. Initially, Pet put great effort into expanding the chain—even putting it in places where W.S. Stuckey had never needed a restroom. Pet was also interested in giving Stuckey's a more identifiable roadside appearance, so the already pointed roofs were swept even taller to become what was referred to as the "cathedral roof" style. They were impressive enough from the outside, but on the interior the cathedral style formed a truly breathtaking A-frame-type ceiling, paneled in shiny hardwood and featuring chandeliers hanging from the peak.

An early 1970s location guide lists Alabama's Stuckey stops as Blount Springs, Cullman and Verbena (all on I-65); Eastaboga (I-20); Fairfax (I-85); and Grand Bay (I-10). Oddly, Stuckey's never had any stores on I-59 in Alabama. And at the time that guide was published, the Stuckey's on U.S. 280 at Sylacauga was the only non-interstate location in the state still operating, no doubt due to the continuing popularity of the Florida Short Route.

Pet eventually grew tired of its acquisition of Stuckey's, which became a victim of overexpansion throughout the country. In response to rising heating and cooling costs, the cathedral ceilings were frequently sealed off with inexpensive drop tile ceilings and fluorescent lighting. The chain was almost dead when Bill Stuckey Jr. reacquired the company in 1985 and reinvigorated it; today, only a handful of Stuckey's remain in Alabama, most of the pre-Pet design but with a couple of the cathedral roofs hanging in there as well.

Now, what of Stuckey's local competitor, Saxon's? Henry and Cora remained true to their origins on the U.S. highways and never developed a very visible interstate presence. When one of their stores did have easy access to an interstate, it was in locations such as Riverside, where one of the final new Saxon's outlets sat at the intersection of U.S. 78 and I-20. The home offices remained in Wellington, where Henry looked after the business end of things and Cora supervised the physical manufacturing of the candy. Difficult as it might be to fathom, Saxon's never used machinery to churn out its goodies; each and every piece was crafted by hand and packaged at the headquarters building.

This successful business model came to a screeching halt in November 1968, when Henry Saxon was tragically killed in an automobile accident. Cora continued her supervision in the candy kitchens, but since she had never been a part of dealing with the chain of stores, she left those up to some of Henry's remaining staffers—who quickly ran the business into the ground just as badly as Pet had done to Stuckey's. Finally, Cora decided to let the stores close as their leases expired, and Saxon's candy would exist only as a specialty item in other gift shops and grocery stores. Cora Saxon lived long enough to see people become nostalgic about the long-ago chain and continued privately making goodies in her own kitchen to give as gifts to her friends and neighbors. She was still working in her kitchen two days before she died at age 102 in June 2010.

Try This Space Suit on for Size

With the failed reminders of Space City, USA, having been ignominiously auctioned off just a short time before, the citizens of Huntsville could have been forgiven if they never wanted to hear about a local attraction with the word "space" in its name again. However, the city had very real ties to NASA and the rest of the U.S. space program, so that theme was to be given a second chance—and this time it would be the real thing, not animated dinosaurs and fairylands.

As we saw, people had been visiting the displays of military hardware at Redstone Arsenal since the late 1950s, but with the coming of the Apollo moonshot programs, the focus had gradually shifted from national defense to the Marshall Space Flight Center operated by NASA. Actually putting astronauts on the moon in July 1969 was the culmination of many years of work, and the timing was perfect for a more comprehensive attraction in the Huntsville area. Opening dates for the U.S. Space and Rocket Center are variously given as the summer of 1969, the fall of 1969 and sometime in 1970. Whichever is correct, it made its debut when space travel was in the news and on visitors' minds.

One pre-opening ad from 1969 used staccato sentences, and lots of periods, to describe the first phase of the new attraction:

> *America's largest missile and space exhibit. 35 acres, 22,000 square feet of display area, 200-seat auditorium.*
>
> *Full-size moon rocket on its side. 363 feet. Saturn 1Bm Jupiter-C. Sergeant. Mercury-Redstone. Gemini-Titan. Lance. Corporal.*
>
> *A piece of the moon, and on it the lunar-landing vehicle and surveyor. Mercury and Gemini capsules that have flown in orbit.*
>
> *Fire a rocket engine. Drive a mobile missile bus. See mice living under simulated space conditions.*
>
> *A space science center owned and operated by the State of Alabama. A monument to an impossible dream.*
>
> *For the price of a ticket, you can call it what you want to call it.*

The Story of Alabama Tourism

After the crude displays at Redstone Arsenal and the never-built Space City, USA theme park, Huntsville finally got it right with this miniature model of the forthcoming Space and Rocket Center in 1969.

Since the space program was far from being finished, exhibits were constantly added over the years. Most of them were permanent, but some were temporary by their very nature. Falling into the second category was Miss Baker, a squirrel monkey that had made the trip into outer space and lived to tell the tail—er, tale. Miss Baker was on hand to greet visitors for the rest of her life, and even after that, her grave is still one of the Space Center's sights to see.

You're Welcome

In at least one aspect, Alabama's tourism industry lagged some twenty years behind a couple of its neighbors. The State of Florida had instituted the novel idea of "welcome centers" in 1949; situated as close to the state line as feasible, one of these structures could be found on each of the major highways that entered the state, giving tourists their first glimpse of the hospitality and array of attraction brochures Florida had to offer. The next state to follow suit was Georgia, but it was the late 1960s before Alabama picked up on the concept. Even then, it was much different than the others.

The first Alabama Welcome Center was at the intersection of I-59 and State Highway 35, near Fort Payne. Granted, by the time travelers entering the state from the north came to that junction, they would have been driving for more than twenty miles, but that was not the only way Alabama's initial welcome center varied from its ancestors.

Wind Creek Park, on Lake Martin, was one of several commercial Alabama attractions that later became part of the ever-growing state park system.

The center was described as a rustic log cabin, the basic structure of which was an 1854 post office. Moved to its convenient location next to the new interstate, this first Alabama Welcome Center was open only from mid-April through Labor Day. Whereas the welcome centers in Florida refreshed their visitors with orange juice, and the ones in Georgia doled out complimentary cups of Atlanta's wondrous creation Coca-Cola, the Alabama welcome center was more of a museum, displaying various artifacts of the 1850s that were donated by DeKalb County residents.

In our next chapter, we shall see how Alabama's welcome centers finally got in stride with their roadside brethren during the 1970s. As for the eventual disposition of the 1854 log cabin that was the original, no one seems to know its fate. Rumors are that it was moved to various locations during its roadside attraction days, and in all likelihood it is still being enjoyed at one of Alabama's northwestern region parks.

THE NEED FOR SPEED

In May 1968, construction began on a new facility in Talladega. Bill France Sr., the founder of NASCAR, had come up with the brilliant idea to build a racetrack in Alabama to counteract the overwhelming number of NASCAR facilities along the East Coast. (Daytona Beach had sired many offspring up and down the Atlantic shoreline.) The site he chose, alongside still-in-progress I-20, was a two-thousand-acre former airfield. Always thinking big, France was determined to out-Daytona Daytona with a track that would be longer, wider and have greater banking in the turns.

No one has to be told that the Alabama International Motor Speedway, as it was called when it hosted its first race in September 1969, was *not* one of the many flops of the state's tourism industry. In fact, it is amazing how on race weekends, a facility devoted to speeding automobiles can convert I-20 into a parking lot.

In 1982, the speedway donated thirty-five acres of its property as a site for the Alabama Motorsports Hall of Fame, which opened in April 1983. It, too, became a top tourist attraction. In 1989, the racetrack changed its name to the Talladega Superspeedway, and it is an impossible sight to miss for those who zip along I-20 between Birmingham and Anniston. Now, if those interstate drivers would only learn to obey the rules like the NASCAR competitors do…

The Old and the New

The 1960s had been a tumultuous decade for Alabama, and an active one for tourism in the state, and at just about the time it was ending there was another flurry of activity involving both old, established attractions and new, hoping-to-be-established ones. Let's first take a look at the changes being wrought in some longtime favorites.

At Noccalula Falls, a movement had begun to give visitors something more to see than just the namesake water plunge. By April 1967, the park had completed the first phase of its "Pioneer Homestead" complex. Just as with the homestead attraction in the Bankhead Forest and the original welcome center, Noccalula's re-created neighborhood was accomplished by disassembling authentic pioneer log structures and faithfully rebuilding them at their new site. Some came from Alabama locations, while others had out-of-state origins. Noccalula historian Danny Crownover related the story of how Gadsden mayor Les Gilliland and park director Ray Bullock located an old homestead in the mountains around Lawrenceburg, Tennessee:

> *They drove their car as far as they could and hiked five miles over the hills to the structures. A sawmill operator was hired to bulldoze and clear a road to the site in order to get the buildings out.*
>
> *The collectors were charged to be careful and not remove items that were considered accessible to the public, or had community value as a landmark. However, this didn't keep any of the mountain folks from blocking the efforts to bring the old structures to Noccalula Park. The promise of shotguns and angry words held the collectors back.*
>
> *Finally, Gilliland and Bullock loaded the old structures onto an almost defunct railroad located nearby. They were then sneaked out of the hills while their defenders were watching the road.*

Besides the new Pioneer Homestead, there was another addition to the park. It seemed rather strange that at a spot called Noccalula Falls, there was no sign of Noccalula (except a snack bar given the arcane name "Noccalula Nik-Nak"). In September 1969, that omission was remedied when the Women's Club of Gadsden unveiled a $25,000 nine-foot bronze statue of the doomed Native American martyr. Sculpted by Suzanne Silvercruys, the petrified princess was installed on a bluff overlooking the falls, caught in mid-stumble just before flinging herself into immortality.

By the 1960s, Noccalula Falls had evolved from a simple Gadsden city park into a true tourist destination. This snack bar with the enigmatic name "Noccalula Nik-Nak" stood ready to help hungry visitors fortify themselves for all the fun in store.

Another metal monarch was about to get a makeover down in Birmingham. Vulcan Park had changed very little since its 1939 grand opening, and with Birmingham's centennial celebration approaching in 1971, there was a feeling that the old place needed a facelift. At the same time the Noccalula statue was being unveiled in Gadsden, bulldozers went to work at Vulcan Park, leveling some of the original structures in preparation for the improvements to come. The park would be closed for more than a year while construction got underway on a new concession building, a new observation platform, a museum and, most importantly from a historical view, an elevator to give folks an alternative to climbing those 159 stairs. In our next chapter, we shall see how these completed modern features came close to ruining the experience they were meant to enhance.

As for new attractions arriving in the state, at least one of them remains a mystery, remembered only for its postcards and ads in the tourism literature of the time. The Muscle Shoals Deer Forest was located on Brighton

Most people already knew the legend of Noccalula, but in 1969 the park dedicated this nine-foot-tall bronze replica of the unfortunate Native American princess, poised as she was just about to end it all and give the falls her name.

The site of the Battle of Horseshoe Bend, near Dadeville, was a national military park, but on nearby U.S. 280, this fort-shaped building housed a miniature diorama where the conflict was acted out over and over all day long. At last report, the structure was serving as a church but retaining its hewn-logs façade.

Avenue ("just three blocks off U.S. 43") and seems to have been a most ambitious and unusual project for that part of the state. Just take a gander, Mother Goose, at its description:

> *Whether seven months or 70 years old, you'll enjoy the animals and the storybook characters along Story Book Lane. In addition to the deer, there are goats, pigs, sheep and other animals. See Jack and the Beanstalk, Humpty Dumpty, Goldilocks, the Three Pigs and their houses, and Jack and Jill. Open from early spring until late fall.*

No further recorded history of the Deer Forest can be found, nor any indication of how long it lasted or what became of its live or fairy tale inhabitants.

If the Deer Forest sounds like a minuscule version of a theme park, consider the plan proposed by the Alabama State Fair Authority in the spring of 1969. This organization announced its plans to build a 630-acre amusement park in Tarrant, with the catchy name of Fair Park East. (The original Fair Park was doing just fine with its Kiddieland collection of rides and other amusements.) There were plans to lease the property, near Jefferson State Junior College, from the Birmingham Water Works Board, but "some legal problems are yet to be solved," the report read. Apparently, they never were, as the plans for Fair Park East finally went south.

We have already seen how the Horseshoe Bend National Military Park was established near Dadeville at the end of the 1950s. It would have been unthinkable for a commercial attraction to try to encroach on the history embedded in that site, but a few miles down U.S. 280, the late 1960s saw the opening of the Battle of Horseshoe Bend, yet another of those indoor miniature landscapes of the Alabama Historama and Chattanooga Confederama type.

No one could accuse the Horseshoe Bend attraction of skimping on its efforts to be impressive. It was touted as the "world's largest battle in miniature," and with its count of three million separate pieces to make it all work, there would have been few to question that claim. The building housing the diorama was a replica of Fort Jackson, an 1814 fortress that played a part in the historic battle. Unfortunately, just as with the fairyland denizens of the Deer Forest, there seems to be no record of what became of the immense Horseshoe Bend diorama. The replica Fort Jackson still stands alongside U.S. 280, most recently serving as a church.

Chapter 4
Slamming on the Brakes

The 1970s was an era when everything seemed to change. Tourism was booming as the decade began, but soon enough there were signs that all was not going to be well. Two major bouts with fuel shortages—one circa 1973 and the other in 1979—made many of those who would normally be vacationing stay at home. And then, as the final months of the 1970s were sputtering to a close, Alabama had an unwelcome visitor that temporarily erased one of its most prominent tourism centers. As the saying goes, fasten your seat belts because it's about to get bumpy.

Canyon Take It?

In states all along the East Coast, particularly New England, New York and New Jersey, the amusement park had a long and illustrious career. For some reason, however, this standby of tourism failed to make any sort of lasting impression in Alabama. As we have seen, the ambitious plans for Space City, USA, crashed and burned as soon they got off the launching pad, and a hoped-for amusement park in Tarrant got lost in the woods. The next attempt to bring traditional amusement-style thrills to the state would also meet an early demise, but at least it outdid the others simply by actually managing to get its gates open in the first place.

Canyon Land Park perched on a bluff overlooking scenic Little River Canyon near Fort Payne. Through this entrance gate awaited a conglomeration of amusement park rides, live music and comedy shows, as well as a complete zoo.

Millard G. Weaver, president of People's Telephone Company, purchased a sixty-acre tract overlooking Little River Canyon, adjacent to the state park of the same name, and on March 8, 1970, opened Canyon Land Park. A prospectus that was prepared while plans for the new park were getting underway demonstrates just how ambitious a project this was conceived to be. Repeatedly, the vitality of the amusement/theme park industry is illustrated by references to Disneyland and the soon-to-be-opened Walt Disney World; in reality, even the most optimistic of the Seven Dwarfs would have found it difficult to draw any sort of comparison between those attractions and Canyon Land Park, other than that they both had parking lots.

Instead, Canyon Land's biggest selling feature was also its most unusual: a chairlift that began at the park's Eberhart Point and descended nearly 1,500 feet into Little River Canyon. Once at the bottom, facilities were provided for swimming, fishing, hiking and picnicking, after which the wet, fishy-smelling, tired and full-stomached tourists could catch the next chair headed back toward the park far above.

And most of the other attractions could be found in that relatively small piece of property on the rim of the canyon. A miniature train "thought it could, thought it could" as it tootled around the landscape. The depot from which it departed was actually the 103-year-old abandoned Collinsville structure, rescued from oblivion by Weaver and converted into a souvenir and gift shop. Amusement rides of the type that could be found in any traveling roadside carnival dotted the property, including bumper cars, the traditional merry-go-round, a Tilt-a-Whirl and a Ferris wheel. Interestingly, when the park's first brochures were printed, none of these elements had yet been built, so those initial advertisements had to make do with artwork of the chairlift and generic photos of the scenery and wildflowers of the surrounding forest.

Over the next few years, Canyon Land Park's features grew to include a zoo with some one hundred animals, plus a variety of live shows ranging from comedy to country music. In July 1972, a local wannabe band known as Wild Country made appearances at the park; the Fort Payne natives later went on to much bigger things as the group known simply as Alabama. But as for the park where they got their earliest exposure, things quickly went downhill even faster than the chairlift could transport visitors to the canyon floor. When Millard Weaver died in October 1973, it signaled the beginning of the end for his park that had begun with such high hopes.

In 1974, the park was purchased by Edward R. Riley, but he soon ran into some unforeseen difficulties, most of them involving the chairlift ride, Canyon Land's main selling point. Inasmuch as the bottom of the chairlift was on state property, permission to alight there depended on an easement that had been granted to founder Weaver. That easement had expired with the sale of the property, and the state was unwilling to renew it unless the "carnival atmosphere" amusements on the canyon rim were removed. Although Governor George Wallace reportedly sent a sworn statement to the effect that he wanted to see the chairlift in operation again, the case dragged on in court well into 1978.

There is scant evidence to indicate just when Canyon Land Park shut down for good, but it must have been sometime between the 1978 court proceedings and the early 1980s. A 1988 newspaper feature gives few clues, except to mention that in 1982 Millard Weaver's son Jackie managed to get the chairlift and some of the surviving rides back into operation. By 1985, the property was for sale, indicating the end had come at some point in the preceding three years.

The main feature at Canyon Land Park was this chairlift that took riders deep into Little River Canyon and then brought them back up again. The miniature train ride was a more earthbound way of touring the property.

Apparently, several of the amusement rides were left in place for years, to rust away among the overgrown weeds and foliage, but some of the chairlift swings have since turned up for sale or display in the area. There is an urban legend that the zoo was disbanded by simply opening the cages and letting the animals escape into the woods, causing people to claim to have seen jaguars and other exotic fauna in the neighborhood for decades afterward. (This unlikely scenario could only exist if some of the zoo animals existed in male/female pairs to propagate their species, of course.)

Eventually, the part of Canyon Land along the canyon rim, from which the chairlift departed, was absorbed into Little River Canyon State Park, and the rest of the property became a campground for a while. In 2012, only a few dilapidated buildings remained on the abandoned site, but the original entrance building and parking lot were still visible. To date, no viable plans have been announced to put the abandoned old facility to any further use, so Canyon Land will have to remain as it is—a curious footnote in Alabama tourism history and another example of how the state seemed ready and able to accept practically any sort of attraction as long as it was *not* an amusement park.

Everything Is Ducky in Decatur

In the summer of 1971, Alabama tourists were introduced to one of the first in what would eventually be a new breed of attraction: the water park. No, it was not at the beach but on a peninsula that jutted out into the Tennessee River at Decatur. Because it was adjacent to the Wheeler Wildlife Refuge, well known for its many temporary and permanent duck-duck-goose residents, the new park was given the name Point Mallard.

While traditional amusement parks depended on mechanical rides to give visitors their thrills, chills and spills, this relatively new concept of a water park based most, if not all, of its attractions on getting people wet and keeping them that way. Foremost in Point Mallard's efforts toward this goal was its most-advertised feature: a wave pool, ostensibly the first in the United States but certainly in the South, which transformed a traditional swim into a simulation of being in the Gulf of Mexico. Such a major undertaking could not have been expected to sit just anywhere, so its surroundings were converted into a sandy beach laden with simulated seaside amenities including a playground, picnic area and (of course) souvenir shops.

If the wave pool were not enough to waterlog Point Mallard's visitors, there was also an Olympic-size swimming pool where the water stayed in one place instead of rolling about. (The pool earned its name when it became the training ground for gold medal–winning diver Jenni Chandler, of the 1976 Olympics.) Back on dry land, there was an eighteen-hole golf course, a campground and tennis courts. Point Mallard's emphasis on water sports must have filled a tremendous void in the tourism world because during its initial season it became the state's most-visited summer-only attraction.

Throughout the rest of the 1970s, Point Mallard's features multiplied like Donald Duck's relatives. A miniature golf course was installed, where the obstacles attempted to give some brief overview into the history of the area. While the wave pool remained front and center, water of the frozen type formed the basis for an outdoor ice-skating rink that gave people a reason to visit the park when it was too cold for any other water activity. And nowhere

Point Mallard Park at Decatur was famed for its wave pool that simulated swimming in the ocean, but it also made generous use of its costumed mascot, Captain Mike Mallard, and plenty of pretty girls in its advertising.

north of Gulf Shores could there be found an Alabama attraction whose brochures pictured so many athletic young ladies clad in their bikinis.

Although Point Mallard could not be considered an amusement park of the type that so often failed in the state, it did eventually fall into one habit most often practiced by that genre. Large and small attractions alike found it valuable to have at least one oversized costumed character on the grounds to help out with entertainment, and Point Mallard had its own contender in the race. The park's mascot was Captain Mike Mallard, a six-foot-tall quacker wearing epaulets and a navy uniform who was prominently featured in the advertising. In the pages that follow, we shall see some other examples of this tried-and-true theme park staple that found a healthy life in attractions of all stripes.

"Moon Over Homewood"

As our last chapter was concluding, we saw Birmingham's literal trademark, Vulcan Park, shut down for a complete overhaul. That process culminated in the October 1971 reopening of the facility, and to the average observer, it might have appeared that the big iron guy was the only part of his namesake attraction that had *not* received a facelift. That would have been very close to correct.

The WPA-era sandstone that covered Vulcan's pedestal was looking outmoded in the eyes of early 1970s beholders, so it was enclosed in a sheath of white marble. That in itself would have been enough to change the park's look considerably, but it was only the beginning. Say what you will about changing times and changing physiques, but by 1971 most people no longer had any burning desire for burning leg muscles after climbing the 159 steps inside the pedestal. (Actually, that number could be doubled if you consider the necessity of coming back down again.) Therefore, as we saw in the previous chapter, plans for Vulcan Park's renovation included an elevator to cut down on tourist fatigue.

The problem was just where to put such a device. Obviously, there was no room inside the pedestal (which tapered from bottom to top anyway), so the only choice was to have a separate elevator shaft alongside the now marble-covered monolith. At the top, the elevator opened into a new observation deck that replaced the original narrow metal platform surrounding the pedestal, just below Vulcan's titanic toenails. As long as they were "improving" things, the planners decided to make the new deck an enclosed affair, complete with ceiling and windows, which did serve a purpose of making it accessible in all sorts of weather. Unfortunately, this new type of observation deck also, for the first time, made it impossible to view Vulcan from anywhere other than on the ground at the bottom. The size of the observation deck, the enlarged pedestal and the extra marble on the outside of the elevator shaft all combined to make Vulcan look smaller—and not being able to see him up close did nothing to help the situation.

Surrounding the base of the pedestal, another building housed a museum of sorts, with display cases attempting to tell the story of Vulcan's evolution from World's Fair exhibit to carnival sideshow attraction to Birmingham's beloved symbol. A covered walkway of 1970s geometric design led to a separate structure that served as a snack bar and souvenir shop. One casualty of the renovations was the hillside of cascading pools and their goldfish, which would have looked out of place in such a modernistic setting. Yet amid all these (sometimes humiliating) changes, Vulcan continued to hold up the 1946 traffic safety torch and stone-facedly—or maybe iron-facedly—ignore the remarks about his bare behind. Since that side of the giant faced the Birmingham suburb to the immediate south of Red Mountain, some local

See Alabama First

Some considered the early 1970s renovation of Birmingham's Vulcan Park to be a horrendous mistake. This marble sheath, enclosed observation deck and adjoining elevator all combined to make the iron giant appear smaller than he actually was. His exposed rear end still mooned the city of Homewood, however.

radio comedians commemorated the view in their satirical song "Moon Over Homewood."

While the Vulcan Park renovation plans were being formulated, there had been some ideas submitted that were impractical for reasons of cost, geography or just plain stupidity. One of them—you can decide which of the above applied—was to have a monorail, of the type pioneered in America by the Disney parks, that would whisk visitors from Vulcan the five miles across town to the zoo and Botanical Gardens. Besides the insurmountable problems that would have been involved (five miles through the air being far different from traversing the same distance on the ground), 1971 was probably not the best time to be trying to get more patrons into the zoo, as that facility was having troubles of its own.

A large number of those problems grew from the zoo's humble beginnings. With very little money to spend, the city had put up somewhat cheap buildings to house the animals and exhibits, and after almost twenty years, they were close to falling apart. For example, the zoo's two elephants were doing their best to destroy their own building and in fact already had their trunks packed. Another problem, which sounds rather odd in light of today's lawsuit-happy society, is that animals and visitors came into frequent contact with one another, which longtime zoo director Bob Truett admitted was against health regulations and inexcusable.

All it took to resolve most of these situations was money, and that, for some reason, never seemed to be overflowing from the city coffers. There was an ambitious ten-year plan that outlined what improvements would be made all the way through 1981; some were and some were not, and other things would get worse before they got better, but today the Birmingham Zoo (Jimmy Morgan's name was dropped after no one remembered who he was) is back on top and listed among the most-visited attractions in the state.

They Needed a Miracle Worker

Some attractions, such as the Birmingham Zoo and Vulcan Park, need occasional renovations to keep them in presentable condition. There are others for which just about any sort of change would invalidate their very reason for existence. When circumstances intervene in the case of the latter type, it can be a traumatic experience for everyone.

This brings us to one of the darkest days in Alabama tourism. On April 8, 1972, an early morning fire all but destroyed Ivy Green and its museum of Helen Keller's life. It seems a crew of painters had left a drop cloth on the floor, and during the night the house's heating unit came on, igniting the paint-stained canvas. The ensuing damage was extensive and, as might be expected, resulted in the loss of many artifacts that, because of their very nature, could not be replaced at any price. One of those was the collection of Keller's childhood dolls—naturally, there could be only one set of those in the world, even if exact duplicates of the antique playthings could be located. An oriental rug that had been a gift to Keller and valued at $10,000 also went up in smoke. As for the furniture in the house, its destruction caused the revelation of a fact that perhaps had not been advertised or promoted widely: they had not been the Keller family's original furnishings but antiques from the same period that had been donated over the years. Therefore, it was entirely possible to obtain additional examples of those items.

Another bright spot was that the fire was confined to the main house and did not affect the small cottage that had been Keller's living quarters after her childhood years. That meant many of the museum pieces illustrating her later life as a writer and public speaker were unharmed.

After six months of intense work, Ivy Green reopened on October 21 and to all appearances was as good as new. Visitors since that time have likely not noticed what no longer exists, and the homeplace continues to exist as a shrine to its internationally famous inhabitant.

Better Than the Average Campground

Some things never go out of style, and for Alabamians, going to the lake was one of those. So it was that in the early 1970s, at least two more parks were developed that used their nearby bodies of water as their main draw—but other than that, their characters could hardly have been more different.

Sportsman's Lake Park was a project of the City of Cullman, and planning was well underway by 1969. The facility was in full swim mode by 1973, with the usual accoutrements of a campground, picnic grounds, fishing pier, miniature train ride and miniature golf course with typically funky obstacles. But among all of these, Sportsman's Lake Park had a secret weapon, which continues to be its emblem even forty years later.

No other park could hope to compete with Sportsman's Lake's resident wildlife. Actually, a more accurate term might be "tamelife." The ducks and geese at the park, conditioned to being fed goodies by tourists all day long, were known to follow their visitors about like affectionate puppies. But while the ducks were causing people to run up a bill, some of the park's less feathery residents were also making waves. The lake for which Sportsman's Lake Park was named was home to catfish, which could be pursued by anglers off the aforementioned pier. But would-be Captain Ds often found that nothing was biting at their hooks because the catfish had learned that by staying close to shore, they would be far more likely to be fed yummy tidbits by non-pole-wielding visitors. If you have never seen a catfish rise to the surface and stick its entire head out of the water to snatch a cracker from your hand, you have never visited Sportsman's Lake Park.

Meanwhile, over on the shores of Lake Guntersville, another park emerged from the realm of television land. In the late 1960s, a Wisconsin entrepreneur, Doug Haag, had gotten the idea to jazz up the traditional family campground by licensing the beloved Yogi Bear cartoon characters and opening a chain of Yogi Bear's Jellystone Park Campgrounds. As franchised affairs, the size and amount of theming varied widely from location to location, but in each case, the property was advertised as more than just a place to park a camper or pitch a tent; they were promoted as true tourist attractions, encouraging people to spend a day even if they could not spend the night.

Guntersville's Jellystone Park, opened in 1972, might not have been the most pared-down of any in the chain, but it certainly had little in common with its franchised brethren in Florida or the West. Statues of Yogi, Ranger Smith, Cindy Bear and Boo Boo dotted the grounds, of course, and the central feature was a large "ranger station" that served as a park office, snack bar, entertainment center and gift shop. Costumed versions of the same characters could be found roaming the grounds at any time, popping in on unsuspecting campers. A miniature golf course was added a few years after the initial opening date, and at dusk, a small drive-in movie theater screen became the site for nightly showings of the classic late 1950s/early 1960s Yogi Bear TV cartoons.

While the Jellystone chain of campgrounds exists to this day, the Guntersville location changed hands around 1980, and all traces of Yogi and his cartoon companions vanished into a bottomless pic-a-nic basket. Today, while the property is still a campground, only a few concrete bases and mysterious metal pipes protruding from the ground show

The national chain of Jellystone Park Campgrounds was based in Wisconsin but established a single location in Alabama on Lake Guntersville during the 1970s. Approaching the main building, campers were greeted by this oversized replica of Yogi Bear and his ever-present pic-a-nic basket.

where the character statues once stood, and the former ranger station is a storage building. Even after thirty years and the erasure of Yogi's name and image, Google maps of Lake Guntersville still indicate that part of the shoreline as Yogi Bear's Jellystone Park, proving that some names never die (or that Google is using some awfully old information to draw its maps).

The State of the Parks

Say, do you know what we haven't checked in on lately? The Alabama State Parks system! After the initial group of eleven parks was established during the 1930s, things had slowed down a bit, with only a few added in each decade since then. The earliest was Lake Guntersville State Park, received as a gift from the lake's creator, the Tennessee Valley Authority (TVA). (When funding is always a problem, free gifts seem to be much appreciated.) The TVA was also the original owner of the land that became Joe Wheeler State Park in 1949.

Some pages ago, we visited the moonshine still in Bankhead National Forest. Well, here is another one, with more hillbillies, that was intended as a surprise sight for those hiking Monte Sano State Park near Huntsville.

During the 1950s, only two parks were added to the state system, Meaher and Lake Lurleen. Things were almost as slow in the 1960s, with Blue Springs State Park joining the gang in 1964 and Lakepoint Resort State Park on Lake Eufaula in 1969. But around that time, there was an important development that would help speed up the process from that point on. The official history explains:

> *In the 1967 regular session, the Alabama legislature passed several pieces of legislation of great significance to the Alabama State Park system. Perhaps the most important of these was Act No. 272, which proposed a constitutional amendment, which was ratified by Alabama voters on December 13, 1967. This amendment authorized the state to issue general obligation bonds in the amount of 43 million dollars, including interest, to be used in construction and development of Alabama State Parks. Act No. 309 of this session imposed a tax on cigarettes to produce revenue to redeem these bonds.*

That brings us back to where we were, in the 1970s. During 1970 alone, Florala State Park and Frank Jackson State Park were developed, and the

We hope whoever placed an order for a supply of these felt pennants ended up getting a break on the price, as they unashamedly pictured that famous Alabama icon "Valcan."

Tannehill State Park was established at the site of Alabama's earliest ironworks in 1972. The Furnace Masters Restaurant was a picturesque place to gobble some grub on the premises.

formerly privately owned Wind Creek Park on Lake Martin was absorbed into the state park family. Buck's Pocket State Park was welcomed in 1971.

Another member to join the clan in 1971 would become one of the most famous of all. In the late 1960s, the Central Alabama District of Civitan International began investigating the possibility of restoring the ruins of the old Tannehill Furnaces into some sort of attraction. Although Birmingham was Alabama's best-known center for iron production, that industry had actually gotten its start about forty years before Birmingham existed, and Tannehill was its birthplace. Located near Bucksville, the 1830 Tannehill Ironworks had played an important role during the Civil War—so important, in fact, that it was destroyed by Union troops in the closing days of that conflict and had existed as heaps of rubble in the woods since then.

Finally, in 1969, the state legislature created the Tannehill Preservation Commission, and after making significant improvements (necessary if visitors were even going to be able to find the place, much less understand what they were seeing), Tannehill State Park had its grand opening on June 5, 1971. Just reaching that goal was an important step because on that day there was not much for people to see except a concession stand and restrooms. It did not stay that way for very long, and through the rest of the decade, additions were made in the form of a miniature railroad, the Furnace Masters Restaurant, a pioneer homestead and petting zoo and many more. In the fall of 1980, the park became the home to the Iron and Steel Museum of Alabama, tracing the long and varied history of that industry.

Perhaps the biggest former commercial attraction to become a state park by osmosis, instead of being built from scratch, was Rickwood Caverns, which left its former life behind in 1974 to become a ward of the state. Except for its traditional red-and-white billboards giving way to the standardized brown-and-white state park signage, there was little apparent change. Since the tour of the caverns remained the centerpiece, and not even the State of Alabama could find a way to make them bigger or create more stalactites, most of Rickwood's extra development came in the surrounding property. Since most similar parks had miniature golf courses, Rickwood added one, too, with a unique twist: instead of motorized windmills or bouncing bowling pins, many of the obstacles at Rickwood's course were the natural rock formations on the property, with the carpeted fairways designed around them for maximum challenge.

The new funds available also made it possible to continue upgrading all the state parks that had been established up to that point. A 1978 ad for the almost ten-year-old Lakepoint Resort called its subject "Alabama's newest Super Park Resort" and described the amenities:

> *It has everything for the perfect family vacation—swimming in indoor and outdoor pools or lake; golf on a championship-caliber 18-hole layout; lighted tennis courts with all-weather surface; great fishing, boating and water skiing, with a complete marina to serve you.*
>
> *Surrounded by stately pines on the lake shore, Lakepoint Lodge has an outstanding restaurant, a coffee shop, cocktail lounge and gift shop, all convenient from the large, beautifully furnished guest rooms.*

Amazing what a little cash transfusion can accomplish, isn't it? But not everyone was so happy about what this abundance of money had wrought. As early as 1972, Cheaha State Park was finishing a $2 million facelift designed to bring more modern conveniences into its Depression-era environment and add a thirty-two-room motel to the existing stone cabins. Reporter Waylon Smithey made the journey up the mountain to check out the progress and was alarmed by what he saw. "The scars it leaves will not heal soon on Alabama's highest mountain," he wrote.

The primary "scars" Smithey saw were the result of clearing timber to put in sewer and power lines. As usual, views differed as to just how permanent the damage was. Park manager Clyde Duncan was of the opinion that in two to five years, one would not even be able to tell where the clearing had been done. Environmentalists, on the other hand, pointed out that the clearing had destroyed a stand of Cumberland azaleas that was one hundred miles south of that species' normal known habitat.

In the end, both sides' arguments had some merit. Whatever "damage" was done must have turned out to be only temporary as far as the public was concerned, though, because while Cheaha is one of the oldest parks in the state system, its observation tower, facilities and unequaled view from the top continue to make it one of the showplaces of Alabama tourism.

My Friend Hernando

At just about the time Rickwood Caverns was retreating from the commercial world into the relative safety of state ownership, another show cave was getting ready to make its debut—for the second time. Howzatagain, you say? Here's how it all came about.

Around 1965, entrepreneurs Fred Layton and Allen Mathis made an attraction out of a cave near Childersburg that, like most of its subterranean brethren, had been a local point of interest for more than a century. Its most salable feature from a tourism standpoint was its huge room filled with beautiful onyx formations, so it was given the name KyMulga Onyx Cave. (KyMulga had been the name of a 1760s Chickasaw village nearby.) Travelers taking the Florida Short Route, U.S. 280, were attracted by constant billboards for KyMulga Onyx Cave, and some of them were even persuaded to stop. Some was not enough, though. In 1969, a newspaper writer from nearby Talladega called on Fred Layton to see what was up down underground, and he took the opportunity to give a slight tongue-lashing to the residents of his own county.

"I'll bet no more than twenty people from Talladega have been in the cave," he grumbled. "The reason is that most men in the Talladega-Childersburg area have been in this cave when they were younger, but they had only a flashlight. They didn't think much of it at the time, so they don't think there's much to it today." He went on to say that the cave had drawn visitors from all over the country, *except* Talladega, Sylacauga and Childersburg.

There was some hope that KyMulga Onyx Cave could benefit greatly from the construction of the Talladega Speedway in 1969, but Layton tempered that optimism: "We're sure the raceway will help, but it won't be a big thing. People coming to the raceway will be interested mainly in racing."

By 1975, Allen Mathis's son and grandson (Allen Jr. and Allen III, if you're keeping score) had taken over operation of the attraction, and they felt they might have put a finger on one element that had kept it from rolling off the general populace's collective tongue: practically no one knew what KyMulga was or how to pronounce it, which was fatal from a marketing standpoint.

With the nation's bicentennial celebration looming, in early 1976 a new name was adopted: DeSoto Caverns. From the beginning, the story had been told that Hernando de Soto had discovered the cave during his 1540 trek across Alabama, and that seemed a good enough reason to name it in his honor. (And every school kid in the state had studied about de Soto in history class, so his name was somewhat of a pre-sold trademark.) Actually, DeSoto Caverns came complete with a whole string of historical claims, any one of which would take a team of historians, archaeologists and anthropologists to prove or disprove, so most visitors were content to take them at face value. Among these was the statement that DeSoto Caverns was the first recorded cave in the United States, when agent Benjamin Hawkins reported it to the newly formed government in 1796. There was certainly no question that it had played an important role in Creek and

KyMulga Onyx Cave was not attracting as many visitors as it hoped with such a difficult name, so in 1976 it became De Soto Caverns and spread its billboards far and wide. Featured prominently was the park's new mascot, Happy Hernando.

Chickasaw tribe legend, and graffiti on the walls indicated that it had been visited by outsiders as early as 1723.

All of that was fine and dandy, but during the 1980s, DeSoto Caverns expanded its customer base by adding a campground, a playground (where the central structure resembled DeSoto's sailing ship), hayrides, panning for gold and gems, a "Lost Trail Maze," a primitive weapons arcade and other such ancillary features. And as we have seen, no self-respecting attraction would have been caught without its own costumed mascot, so DeSoto Caverns introduced the cheerful Happy Hernando. He could be found greeting visitors in person on site and grinning widely at potential customers from the plethora of billboards that DeSoto Caverns continued to spread across eastern Alabama.

All the publicity helped bring the attention that Fred Layton had been so desperately seeking a decade earlier. In the early 1980s, motion picture production was added to the many other claims made by DeSoto Caverns. United Artists chose the giant Onyx Cave as the location for a horror picture, *King Cobra*, where a giant mechanical snake used the glittering setting as his/its "throne room." A more prosaic use of DeSoto Caverns was for the 1982 CBS-TV movie *The Further Adventures of Tom Sawyer and Huck Finn*. Even ten years later, the props and sets built for these productions were still being advertised as part of the regular caverns tour.

Welcome, Neighbor

Although, as we have seen, the "log cabin" welcome center at Fort Payne had existed as far back as the late 1960s, the state Welcome Centers Department does not consider that one as an official part of its history. Instead, it dates the first real Alabama Welcome Center to August 11, 1974, and the opening of the facility on I-10 at Grand Bay, near the Mississippi state line. The next welcome center was not far behind, on U.S. 231 at the Florida state line.

Things really kicked into high gear in the latter half of the decade. Just in time for the busy 1977 tourist season, Alabama added two new welcome centers at its state lines. In May, the one on I-65 at Ardmore made ready to welcome drivers entering from Tennessee with open arms, and in August, its sister center on I-85 at Lanett would do the same for inbound traffic from Georgia. In 1978, construction began on an I-59 welcome center in DeKalb County, only much closer to the state line than the log cabin in

The Alabama welcome centers raised a few eyebrows by having monuments bearing the state motto, "We Dare Defend Our Rights." Although some people thought the motto smacked of an earlier era, it still appears in front of the welcome centers today.

Fort Payne had been. Among all the jubilation, however, there was evidence of the coming days when seemingly nothing could be done without raising some sort of controversy—no matter how benign it might seem.

The trouble started at the I-65 welcome center. On the lawn in front of the building was a simulated stone marker bearing the Alabama state motto. Nothing wrong with that, right? Not according to the state highway department. There was a feeling that, after years of trying to live down the more troubling aspects of its past, the last thing people entering Alabama from the north needed to see was a sign proclaiming, "WE DARE DEFEND OUR RIGHTS."

So what if that happened to be the official state motto? Some of North Alabama's tourism promoters felt that it smacked heavily of "states' rights" and the whole "stand in the schoolhouse door" debacle of fifteen years before. It probably did not help matters that the governor who made that infamous stand, George Wallace, was governor once again, and he took what seemed to be almost personal offense at the idea that anyone would object

The Story of Alabama Tourism

to the slogan. Two weeks after the I-65 welcome center opened, highway department crews were preparing to cover the motto with a bronze plaque bearing the state tourism department's current slogan, "Alabama Has It All." But from the governor's mansion in Montgomery, Wallace put up a stop sign.

"They're not going to cover it over. Anybody who doesn't like it can just walk on," he told reporters, sounding vaguely like this sort of argument had come up before. "It hasn't stopped anybody from coming into the state. Alabama is full of tourists. I think the motto embodies the spirit of the people of Alabama. We have dared defend our rights, and that's one of the reasons all the people are coming into Alabama today." Apparently, enough people agreed with Wallace because the marker with the state motto still proudly squats near the front entrance.

There was no such controversy at the I-85 welcome center, perhaps because most of the traffic stopping there was entering by way of Georgia. Even at that, it attracted a quite diversified population of tourists. During the center's first day of operation, attendants reported serving visitors from Virginia, North Carolina, Tennessee, Texas and Maryland. Even foreign countries were represented, with delegates from British Columbia and Sweden getting into the act. And, reported the news articles,

> *a motorcycle rider from Sydney, Australia was helped on his way, while the daughter of a couple from Copenhagen, Denmark listened in fascination to the "Talking Map" as it reported on places of interest in Alabama—although she did not understand a word of English.*
>
> *Located in the Governor's Lounge in a carpeted area adjoining the standup counter and information center, the Talking Map is waist high and contains a large Alabama map divided into seven regions. Each region has its own color lights that shine when a visitor picks up one of the red telephones and pushes a button in the region in which he is interested. He then receives information on the tourist attractions there.*

Controversy had not ended with the state motto. In addition to that monument, each welcome center also displayed all of the different flags that had flown over Alabama during the state's history—and you guessed it, one of those happened to be the Confederate flag. That would have been enough to get plenty of people's dander up, but then the question arose of just *which* Confederate flag, if any, would be flown. Until 1993, it was the "battle flag," the one most people think of as the only Confederate flag thanks to its frequent use (or misuse) by the Ku Klux Klan and the Dukes of Hazzard. Governor Jim Folsom (son of the governor who had played such a large role in Alabama's immediate post–World War II tourism growth) decreed that the offending battle flag be replaced by the "Stars and Bars," the first Confederate flag, which bore absolutely no resemblance to its much-maligned cousin.

By 1996, Fob James was the governor, and he waded right into the mêlée with both feet. He opined that since the Stars and Bars had never officially been adopted as the Confederate flag, due to its close similarity to the United States flag, the welcome centers should fly the real Confederate flag—which just happened to have the battle flag emblem in its upper left-hand corner. That decision pleased no one, as both battle flag buffs and those who wanted no Confederate emblems represented at all gave James equal grief over the situation. However, it was apparently the only choice, since that flag (which, incidentally, became official only a month before the South surrendered) is still the one representing that era at each welcome center.

Regardless of what flags were or were not flying over them, this new generation of welcome centers also featured a ten-minute video about the state's attractions, brochures in seventy-eight racks on each side of the room, and oversized color photos of the most spectacular of the attractions. Whether someone was coming to stay in Alabama overnight, for a few days or for the rest of their life, the welcome centers had developed into the ideal way to say, "Howdy, y'all…come on in an' set a spell."

They'll Never Pay That

For the most part, the summer of 1979 was the low point in the nation's tourism industry. The first big sock in the jaw had been the oil embargo of the early part of the decade. Gas prices had soared, but just finding a service station that was open for business was a challenge because of the fuel shortage. With the recession that hit in the closing years of the 1970s, the situation returned, and this time some who had been in the business for years felt they could no longer continue.

Stations and drivers everywhere, including in Alabama, were dismayed when, in June 1979, the price of a gallon of gas skyrocketed to the outrageous level of ninety-nine cents per gallon. One service station owner between Opelika and Phenix City chose to close up shop before he would stoop to charging such extravagant prices. Another station owner on U.S. 280 put up a sign announcing that instead of his customary 11:30 p.m. closing time, he would begin shutting things down at 8:00 p.m. "because of illness in government." He imposed a limit of five dollars on purchases of regular gas and ten dollars on unleaded gas.

For all the hubris over the fuel situation, Alabama's tourist attractions fared a little better than ones in other parts of the South, since they did not depend so heavily on out-of-state visitors. For example, while the indefatigable Rock City on Lookout Mountain was having its worst summer ever, Tannehill State Park was announcing that it was setting new records in its attendance figures. People were staying closer to home, and that was a good thing for Alabama—even if not so much for Tennessee or Georgia or Florida. Alabama was about to get its own whipping, though, so while we wait for that story, be sure to get in your time machine and go back to 1979, where you can snicker at the people who thought ninety-nine cents per gallon was too much to pay for gas. If they had only known, they would have been dancing in the streets.

Nature's Eraser

Just as the expensive 1979 summer season was drawing to a close, a force that was completely out of the control of the government or anyone else did its part to reshape a major part of Alabama's tourist industry. Before getting into that, we need to take a look at what had been going on along the state's relatively short stretch of Gulf Coast since the last time we looked in on the region.

Over on Dauphin Island, most of the development had been in the form of motels and their attendant businesses: restaurants, service stations and beach supply stores. There were no real commercial amusements of the type found in most beach resorts, but that did not keep people from enjoying the water and the sand and, of course, faithful old Fort Gaines holding down the, well, fort.

At Gulf Shores, things were a bit livelier. The perceived model was Florida's Miracle Strip resorts of Fort Walton Beach and Panama City Beach, which, combined with Pensacola Beach and the Alabama coast, had long earned its nickname of "Redneck Riviera." If Panama City Beach seemed to embody all that was tacky in seaside amusements, Gulf Shores

By the 1970s, Gulf Shores had developed into a lower-budget version of Florida's Miracle Strip resorts. Here, in 1973, we see one of the more unusual attractions, Spooky Golf (also known as Surfside Golf).

was determined to emulate it...but with less investment capital, it ended up looking like a somewhat half-hearted attempt.

Throughout the 1960s, Gulf Shores had remained steadfastly tiny. Small mom-and-pop motels and cabins crouched among the sand dunes, and restaurants were as low key as the rest. By the early 1970s, growth had begun to sputter along the beach, with a four-story Holiday Inn arriving in 1971 to make everyone gasp at its luxury. The Friendship House Restaurant, on Highway 59 north of Gulf Shores, had the unusual feature of an antique store built into its premises. As a local guidebook phrased it, "Along the beaches can be seen dozens of motels and restaurants, bait and tackle shops and places where visitors can find unusual souvenirs to take home." (A bit of irony: those dinky souvenirs of the late 1960s and early 1970s would now be valuable additions to the inventory of the Friendship House's antique shop.) The same guidebook enumerated that Gulf Shores was home to three hundred business licenses, which included seven restaurants, nine drive-ins and fast-food eateries, seven grocery stores ("most of which sell beach supplies and related items"), six service stations and two marinas.

Whereas Panama City Beach made a lasting impression on hundreds of thousands of visitors with its Miracle Strip Amusement Park and Goofy Golf, Gulf Shores took its own humble approach to both concepts. There was a gloriously homemade-looking miniature golf course that bore the name "Spooky Golf" on its signage. Apparently, at some point in the early 1970s, the property was merged with an adjacent RV park, and both the park and golf course became known as "Surfside." Under either name, Spooky/Surfside Golf was a terrific example of the concrete-and-chicken-wire method of constructing miniature golf obstacles. Its roadside lure was a towering purple dinosaur with red light bulb eyes that lit up at night.

Down the street was Gulf Shores's attempt at an amusement park, but if this collection of rides ever had an official name, those in the community who should know such things have forgotten it. The park had its own miniature golf course, with obstacles constructed of wooden flats rather than concrete, but it is largely forgotten today except as a hazy memory by kids who played there. The nameless amusement park would soon be joined by a lot of other businesses as hazy memories as well.

People generally think of Gulf Shores as having two distinct eras: the period of time before September 13, 1979, and everything since. For it was on that night that Hurricane Frederic, a Category 3 storm, roared ashore from the Gulf, bringing a new look to the area—and initially, it was not a pleasant one. Firsthand witness Emmett Burnett colorfully described what took place during that blackest of black nights:

> *Locals heard sounds of metal crashing, trees snapping and buildings falling. No one saw the mayhem taking place in the wee hours. The storm was physically huge, an eye-stretching forty miles wide. Before weather instruments were obliterated, Dauphin Island recorded wind speeds of 147 miles per hour.*
>
> *County roads in and around coastal areas were covered in debris and fallen trees. The forty-minute drive from Citronelle to Saraland was now an eight-hour trip. Dauphin Island was cut in half, with nothing man-made left unscathed. The lone bridge connecting the island to the mainland was no more.*

Indeed, the cost of Hurricane Frederic had to be measured in its devastating effect on the lives of the people who lived on the coast, from

Virtually every man-made business in Gulf Shores was obliterated by the landfall of Hurricane Frederic in September 1979. Small cinder-block motels and goofy miniature golf courses would thereafter be replaced by upscale condominiums and restaurants.

Gulf Shores to Mobile, with the health of the tourism industry as a mere afterthought (if thought about at all). But it was not long before those who had staked their lives on those visiting tourists began to think about what it was going to take to bring them back—and a conscious decision was made to cater to a quite different type of tourist than in the BF (Before Frederic) epoch.

Dauphin Island would never be quite the same again. It had been wiped almost clean, and much of it to this day remains in its forcibly reverted natural state. The man-made attractions around Mobile Bay had to clean up their acts, too. Both Bellingrath Gardens and the USS *Alabama* had to be closed while damage was assessed and repairs made. The gardens suffered the most, having to be closed for six months. An estimated $6 million in damages affected the Bellingrath home and the surrounding acreage, where nearly three thousand trees were destroyed or crippled. A spokesperson for the attraction revealed that the gardens were, out of necessity, "being redesigned to take advantage of sun instead of shade."

At Battleship Memorial Park, the hurricane had done what enemy warfare could not and caused the USS *Alabama* some nicks and scratches, mainly to a plane that was mounted on a catapult on the ship's stern. The USS *Drum* submarine fared worse; the newspapers reported, "She pulled loose from her moorings and was pounded by the waves into her own gangways. It will take some time to repair her."

The worst damage, and thus the greatest transformation, was reserved for Gulf Shores. Herbert Malone, president of the Gulf Shores Convention and Visitors Center, put it in no uncertain terms: "Before the hurricane, we were a land of mom-and-pop cabins, cinder-block hotel cottages and cheeseburger stands. But after the storm, we grew up." People who owned property that once contained a motel, a restaurant or Spooky Golf suddenly found themselves in possession of a completely blank slate, with hungry developers slobbering to sink their fangs into it. Five years after Frederic, Gulf Shores could boast five thousand condominium and hotel rooms—more than the entire population of the town before the storm. Today, estimates are that the town has at least sixteen thousand rooms, with more on the way all the time.

For anyone familiar at all with today's Gulf Shores (and Orange Beach, which sometimes threatens to take over the neighborhood), it need not be pointed out that most of those rooms are not in hotels and motels but in condominiums. Just as it is along Florida's Gulf Coast, the leaders on Alabama's shoreline decided it was time to retire the old "Redneck Riviera" image and concentrate on the more upscale brand of tourist. Today's Alabama Gulf Coast has the amusements that it lacked during the pre-Frederic era, and for the most part, those who are not particularly nostalgic will assure anyone that the quality of life is much improved. There are a few folks, however, who still miss the four-story Holiday Inn, and Spooky Golf and the Amusement Park Without a Name and wonder just how many pieces of them still rest at the bottom of the Gulf.

REST STOP

After Richard Hail Brown got out of the Holiday Inn business, he started his own chain of motels known as Hiway Host. This particular example could be seen on U.S. 231 at Ozark. *Mike Cowart collection.*

Top: The La Capri was a terrific example of the typical small (in this case, thirty-six rooms) motels that were built on Dauphin Island in the 1950s. As in Gulf Shores, practically all such commercial development was erased by Hurricane Frederic in 1979.

Bottom: Folks who were passing through Montgomery and spotted this neon sign for Doby's Hotel Court knew for certain that they were not in New York or Chicago. Doby's went even further and splashed this cartoony colonel on every piece of furnishing in the rooms. *Warren Anderson collection.*

The Story of Alabama Tourism

Above: In the late 1960s, Hartselle became the headquarters for a new chain of franchised restaurants, Branded Burgers. They did not last long, but the rotating fiberglass hamburger perched on the roof made for an unforgettable visual symbol.

Left: In the days before Kentucky Fried Chicken had its own stand-alone outlets, the tasty treat was featured as a menu item at dozens of independent restaurants across Alabama and the rest of the nation. Bergeron's in Huntsville was but one example of these.

SHERER'S
SELF-SERVICE
RESTAURANT

North of Jasper

OPEN — 8 A.M. TILL 11 P.M.
7 DAYS

- Carry Out Service
- Box Lunches
- Seat Up to 100
- Welcome All Ages

For Carry Out Service —

Call **387-1484**

3107 8 HWY BY-PASS, W.

Another drive-in chain with locations throughout Alabama, from the Tennessee line all the way down to Ozark, was Sherer's. The chain's distinctive A-frame building with maroon and yellow stripes on the front was an immediately identifiable trademark.

Chapter 5
Proceed with Caution

The 1980s and '90s brought both good and bad to Alabama's tourism industry. With the recession of the last decade receding, people took to the highways again, and new attractions began opening once more. But the tourist business is a fickle one; some of those new enterprises survived to take their places among all the established ones, while others crashed and burned in impressive blazes of glory. We shall now take a look at both types—and you might want to hold your breath as you try to figure out which ones are going to turn out which way!

How the West Was Won—and Lost Again

Many pages ago, we visited the short-lived Dry Gulch Ghost Town that attempted to bring to Gardendale the genre of western attraction that had proven successful in so many other tourist areas. There is no way to know just how long Dry Gulch might have staked its claim along U.S. 31 had it not burned to the ground, but a decade later, it was time for someone else to try the theme again. Perhaps the best way to start is with a press release:

> *In 1980, Herb Collett, manager of American Legion Post 170 of Ashville, Alabama, met Carney Waller, an Alabama native who was a retired set builder and artist who worked for many years helping create the sets for Western movies.*

> *During his lifetime, Waller traveled all over the West and worked on the sets of many western movies, where he met and became friends with some of Hollywood's most famous cowboys. Two of his most notable friends were John Wayne and Ken Curtis. One of the best-known movie sets he helped create was for John Wayne's movie Rio Lobo. Carney Waller was also an accomplished painter of western scenes and cowboy life.*
>
> *Legiontown USA is the result of the dream of Herb Collett and Carney Waller to re-create the Old West right here in Alabama. Although Waller is now deceased, the dream lives on here in Legiontown through his excellent work.*

Yes. Legiontown, USA, was the latest attempt to bring the Wild West to the Deep South. Its location was on U.S. 11, seven miles south of Steele and very near the major intersection of 11 and U.S. 231. The proximity to Horse Pens 40 certainly helped, and by 1981, Legiontown, USA, was attracting its share of visitors, if not necessarily as many as its cousin parks Ghost Town in the Sky in North Carolina and Six Gun Territory in Florida.

There was an unwanted similarity between Legiontown, USA, and the long-forgotten Dry Gulch Ghost Town, too. On April 6, 1982, a fire swept through the ersatz town, reducing it to charred ashes within thirty minutes. Within two days, the members of the American Legion Post had voted to rebuild it, and this time they were determined to make it better than ever.

One reason the fire had consumed the attraction so quickly was that the buildings had all been constructed of wood. None of them had a second floor, although a few had false fronts to give the impression of a two-story structure. The new Legiontown, USA buildings would be more substantial, built from concrete block but with the traditional wooden western façades to preserve character. And speaking of characters, both the old and new versions of Legiontown, USA, had quite a cast of them, ranging from dance hall girls to the gunfighters who shot it out with the marshal in the street several times a day to the always comical undertaker who got laughs with his not-so-subtle attempts to increase his own business. Before the fire, Legiontown, USA, had been a favorite hangout for longtime Birmingham TV personality Country Boy Eddy, and the rebuilt attraction would boast the Country Boy Eddy Museum, displaying much of the memorabilia the entertainer had gathered during his career.

For a park that was always considered a fundraiser for the American Legion to carry on its charitable work, there were some grandiose plans for

With Gardendale's Dry Gulch Ghost Town long since having bitten the dust, in 1980 Legiontown, USA, opened on U.S. 11 near Ashville. For a few years, it carried on the tradition of dance hall girls and outlaws shooting it out with the marshal in the streets.

Legiontown, USA. There were hopes of eventually adding such rides as a roller coaster, Ferris wheel and log flume. Construction got underway on a walk-through "gold mine"/haunted house type attraction. There was even talk of a movie theater where the classic black and white western movies would be shown. So what happened?

Legiontown, USA, was still going, and hoping to go further, in 1988, but all records of it seem to end around that time. Driving past the American Legion Post 170 today, one sees mostly signs for bingo. But take a closer look; behind the building, the structures of Legiontown, USA, still stand along a formerly dusty western street that is now overgrown with weeds. Somehow, it looks very much like what it was always intended to resemble: a genuine western ghost town, where the spirits of John Wayne, Festus and the Lone Ranger still whisper in the wind as it blows through the buildings' open doors.

Water, Water Everywhere

In the previous chapter, we saw how Point Mallard was at the front of the V formation when it came to predicting the eventual mania for water-based amusement parks. That enthusiasm for soaking visitors would grow throughout the 1980s, but one of the first Alabama attractions to see it coming was Water World, which opened in Dothan on May 3, 1980.

It did not take much observation to determine that Water World was conceived as a South Alabama parallel to Point Mallard. In fact, most of its opening day publicity gave full credit to its Decatur inspiration. It seems that as far back as September 1974, a contingent from Dothan's chamber of commerce had made an overnight trip to Point Mallard to observe the legendary wave pool and had returned home with the determination—if not the available funds—to do the same in their own community. The city already had a suitable piece of property, which had been the Dothan airport from the 1930s until 1965, but it took until 1979 before construction could begin.

Once Water World was ready to open, the city greeted it as if Walt Disney himself had come back to life and built a theme park in the vicinity. A whole series of publicity photos featured the current Miss Dothan, Tracy Young, in a breathtaking assortment of poses. With her cutoff bluejean shorts, Young definitely appeared to be channeling TV sensation Daisy Duke, but she let it be known that she was a licensed lifeguard, so her publicity shots taken around the wave pool were more than mere posing.

Naturally, the Point Mallard–inspired wave pool was Water World's biggest selling feature. Pains were taken to point out that, other than Decatur, the next nearest such water attractions were at Ocala, Florida (where Wild Waters had been grafted onto the veteran Silver Springs), and Orlando (where Wet and Wild was ducking tourists who were in the neighborhood to visit with Donald). But coming in for almost as much attention was Thrill Hill, a giant water slide with three four-hundred-foot flumes, each of which culminated in a splash pool. Overlooking the wave pool was a light tower to provide illumination for night swimming.

Dothan's enthusiasm for Water World was evidenced by the lavish thirty-six-page section the local newspaper devoted to promoting the grand opening. Water World and Point Mallard were unique, but not for long, as within a decade water parks would become an indispensable part of any summer-oriented tourist area.

One might pause to wonder why a water park would be needed when the entire Gulf of Mexico was next door, but such was the case of Gulf Shores'

Dothan's Water World was patterned after Point Mallard in Decatur and opened in the spring of 1980. Its pre-opening publicity photos benefited greatly from the presence of that year's Miss Dothan, Tracy Young, seen posing here with some of her young admirers.

Waterville, USA, which opened in May 1987. Like Point Mallard and Water World, it featured a wave pool—somewhat redundantly, one would think. But for those who preferred artificial waves to the real thing, Waterville, USA, was there to fill the need.

In Fairhope, yet another water park got started at about the same time as these other projects, but it had a much different ending. Perhaps someone should have seen trouble ahead when it was given the name Styx River Water World; surely there were better ways to get attention than naming it after the mythical river that served as the dividing point between life and death.

Without the heart-stopping good looks of Dothan's Tracy Young, Styx River Water World had to attract attention in other ways. It cast its lot with a large collection of oversized fiberglass statues of various humans and animals scattered over the property, like a miniature golf course that had grown beyond its borders. A 1990s brochure put these immobile immortals front and center, both literally and figuratively:

> *When pulling into our free parking lot, you can't miss Clem, a 20-foot-tall farmer and his steer (or is it a bull?). Then you see Big Tex, the overgrown cowboy, and you know that you have discovered "a very unusual water park." Bring your camera to take pictures of your family and friends with the many Styx River Water World mascots.*

Perhaps the most unusual thing about Styx River Water World was its fate. For reasons unknown, the whole facility seems to have shut down in 2001. Since then, the continually deteriorating ruins of the attraction have gained somewhat legendary status among roadside history buffs. An Internet search for the attraction's name turns up multiple websites where people have ventured into the overgrown and abandoned property to try to capture some images of what is left. Putting them into chronological order, it seems that in the mid-2000s, most of the fiberglass statues still existed in one form or another but that by 2010, there was nothing left but piles of rubble. It took awhile, but it appears the last remnants of Styx River Water World have finally crossed that river from which its name was derived.

Another water-based attraction, though not exactly of the same type as Point Mallard and Water World, was Tom Mann's Fish World on U.S. 431 north of Eufaula. Famous fisherman Mann had moved his anglers' supply manufacturing company to the area in the late 1960s and, by the 1980s, had expanded into an aquarium that was reminiscent of many such Florida roadside stops of the past. The star attraction was Leroy Brown, the largemouth bass Mann caught in 1973 and did not have the heart to eat. (He remained the baddest fish in the whole Mann town.) After Leroy went on to fish heaven from natural causes in 1981, his grave became part of the attraction. Both Mann and his Fish World joined Leroy in the afterlife in 2005, but the monument to Tom Mann's finny friend can still be seen on the former property.

Forging Ahead

Tourists driving through Birmingham in 1980, whether on one of the still partially completed interstates or on one of the older highways that continued to serve as backup, saw a skyline quite different from the past. The 1970s had produced a boom in skyscraper construction, meaning the old City Federal Building and Thomas Jefferson Hotel no longer towered above everything else. One of the even more noticeable changes, though, was that the skyline could actually be seen.

Increased federal regulation concerning air pollution had had a numbing effect on what was once Birmingham's claim to fame: its blast furnaces. Some were able to comply with the new rules for a time, while others simply stopped iron and steel production in their tracks. One of the latter had been the Sloss Furnaces, which traced its origins back to 1882. After shutting down in 1970, Sloss became a rusting collection of buildings and smokestacks behind a chain-link fence, with weeds overtaking the property.

There were some stirrings of activity during 1976, when the first surveys were done to document Sloss's historic authenticity. The surveys showed that even though everyone knew of Sloss's heritage as one of Birmingham's first steel mills, nothing remained of its original 1882 construction. Since it had been a working plant all those years, its various elements had been updated as the needs of steelmaking changed. There were some parts that dated back to 1902, but most of the existing structure was built in the 1920s and 1930s. It was still historic enough to be impressive, and plans began swirling around about just what could be done about developing it for tourism purposes.

In 1977, a bond issue was passed by Birmingham voters, allotting some $3.3 million for the Sloss project. But there it seemed to mire in the mud that now surrounded the abandoned facility. Exactly *what* should it be? Initial ideas called for a museum, but as the 1970s became the 1980s, the always popular (and in Alabama, frequently toxic) term "theme park" was being bandied about. As we saw in our last chapter, 1979–80 was hardly the best time to be contemplating a new entry in the never-ending tourism road race, and there were those who felt the Sloss project was going to end up as, instead of a monument to Birmingham industry, a monumental bottomless pit of expense.

In 1980, WAPI-TV news director Wendell Harris made his views clear in an on-air editorial devoted to the topic:

> *Our city leaders and the rest of us got a first real look at the proposed Sloss Furnace project this week. It will combine government money with funds from private industry to create a theme park at the old steelmaking facility. While my first reaction is to advise that it be scuttled, I want to be reasonable about it. I think it would be better at this time to put the Sloss Furnace project on the far back burner. We are having economic bad times; city revenues are down; direct services to citizens are being cut back. All of us probably know someone who is being laid off or facing financial*

Birmingham's Sloss Furnaces were among the earliest of that city's legendary steel mills. After being shut down in 1970, the property sat vacant and overgrown with weeds before being turned into an outdoor museum in 1983.

difficulty because of the recession. Just those reasons alone are enough to put a deep freeze on the Sloss Furnace project, but I have one more thing to be considered.

Why can't the project be financed by industry and other private sources, when it has recovered from the recession and times are good? Where does it say we must look to government—city, state, or national—for money for projects? If industry supports the Sloss Furnace project, as I am told it does, then those supporting the effort should look to industry for financial backing, and not to taxpayer dollars.

The darkened furnaces of Sloss began looking just a bit brighter, at least symbolically, when the facility was designated a National Historic Landmark in 1981. There might have been hope that its new career as a tourist draw would begin in time for its centennial in 1982, but development stretched into the following year, with an official opening date in September 1983. No, it was not the theme park some people wanted and others feared but a well-preserved museum to educate visitors on the steelmaking heritage that had forged the city of Birmingham out of the area's raw materials.

Coal Miners and Cowboys

In the 1980s, it seemed that just about any community that wanted a museum of some sort could have one, as long as there was a building to house it and locals who were willing to donate artifacts. Such museums, localized by their very nature, became a terrific way to learn more about a town's history than, say, driving through on the highway and grabbing a burger at the local McDonald's. One typical facility that grew out of such thinking was in far eastern Walker County, barely over the Jefferson County line.

That part of the state was coal-mining country, and dozens of small towns had been born and prospered because of that black, dusty stuff. Likewise, many of those same towns had seen their prosperity dry up when the mines closed. Some withered away completely, to be seen only as crumbling buildings in the middle of nowhere. The town of Dora was a bit more fortunate, as just about the time coal mining was on the decline, most of the local business was moving from the original center of activity to the four-lane U.S. 78. Dora developed a somewhat Jekyll-and-Hyde split personality, with a modern shopping center and chain restaurants on the highway and an almost-forgotten former downtown area along a weedy main street that resembled Legiontown, USA, without the cowboys.

In the early 1980s, some townspeople got together and decided that the region's coal-mining legacy was too important to be forgotten, so after much work, the Alabama Mining Museum opened in September 1984. Even its facility came with a historic pedigree: it was the former Dora High School gymnasium, one of the many stone-faced buildings constructed during the WPA era. The high school having moved to the "new part" of town in the late 1960s, the empty gym was looking a bit neglected, and the Mining Museum filled the bill (and its cavernous interior).

Locals from eastern Walker and western Jefferson Counties contributed relics and photos from the area's coal-mining legacy, but the museum was not confined to the interior of the ex-gym. Soon, the surrounding grounds were home to a number of transplanted historic buildings, including a railroad depot, a one-room school and even the engine of one of the locomotives that had hauled coal to its faraway markets.

The Alabama Mining Museum still welcomes visitors, although it must be admitted that it never made it onto the major state attractions maps. Perhaps this was inevitable because its location in the "forgotten" part of Dora means it has faced the same problems with accessibility as the businesses that once surrounded it. For those who care to get off the main highway, it can truly be a journey into the past.

Another museum of a vastly different type certainly had no such problem with accessibility during its brief life; perhaps, if anything, overenthusiasm was the reason for its downfall. Jesse Rush was a lifelong western movie fan who had cultivated a close personal friendship with crooning cowpokes Gene Autry and Roy Rogers, along with many of their silver screen saddle pals, over the years. Rush had amassed a truly staggering collection of vintage western movie posters, toys, records, sheet music and anything and everything else connected with the genre and (as happens so often in such cases) needed a place to keep and display it all.

In March 1986, he opened the American Cowboy Heroes Museum in Boaz. Since that town had long ago developed into a tourist destination because of its outlet stores, there were plenty of potential visitors. Rush's museum hitched up its cowboy britches and moseyed into one of the vacant storefronts to sit a spell and chew the fat with anyone who cared to drop in. It was laid out with meandering hallways, each filled with memorabilia but leading to open rooms containing even more display cases of the colorful

Among the many museums that opened in Alabama during the 1980s was the short-lived American Cowboy Heroes Museum in Boaz. Winston County native Pat Buttram was on hand for the grand opening ceremonies in the spring of 1986.

pop culture artifacts. One room was a re-created movie theater, where the black-and-white films played out on a screen in a continuous loop.

Even though Rush prevailed upon his old buddy Pat Buttram (Gene Autry's former movie and TV sidekick, as well as Mr. Haney of *Green Acres*) to preside over the grand opening day, the American Cowboy Heroes Museum failed to attract the attention of enough people who were in Boaz to shop for bargains, not to look at priceless collectibles. One has a feeling that even if Rush had changed it from a museum to an antique store, the typical Boaz tourist would not have been willing to pay what the western mementoes were going for on the collectors' market. So, just like the film stars it memorialized, after just a few years the American Cowboy Heroes Museum saddled up and rode off into the sunset.

These were only a couple of examples of museums that opened during the 1980s. For the rest of that decade, and throughout the 1990s, museums seemed to become almost a cottage industry in Alabama (and some of them really were located in cottages). Probably no one could compile a definitive list of all the museums that have operated in the state, but here we will try to acknowledge enough of them to give a reasonable view of the variety they provided.

Since so many towns in Alabama, large and small, owed their existence to the railroad, it should not be surprising that a number of them had museums devoted to the subject—frequently located in the former town depot. The North Alabama Railroad Museum in Huntsville and the Heart of Dixie Railroad Museum in Calera were a couple that preserved the days of riding the rails. History of widely varying other epochs could be sampled at the American Village (Montevallo), the Air Force Enlisted Heritage Hall (Montgomery), the Alabama Rural Heritage Center (Thomaston), the Alabama River Heritage Museum (Monroeville), the Choctaw County Historical Museum (Gilbertown), the Scottsboro-Jackson Heritage Center (Scottsboro) and the Berman Museum of World History (Anniston). The Old Courthouse Museum in Monroeville staged an annual performance of *To Kill a Mockingbird*, part of which was set in the courthouse's earlier days.

With Alabama being as addicted to sports as any state you could find, the Alabama Sports Hall of Fame found a welcome home in Birmingham. And if anyone did not know the Paul W. "Bear" Bryant Museum could be seen in Tuscaloosa—well, as the old folks would say, bless their heart. Children's museums were another phenomenon that rose to power during the 1980s and 1990s; the Sci-Quest Science Center in Huntsville encouraged kids to touch things, in a reversal of most museums' policies, while those same kids might have had a cow if their parents refused to let them visit the MOOseum in Montgomery. Even I began my own museum in the early 1980s—but that is quite literally another story for another book.

Righting a Wrong

A couple of chapters ago, we had a brief reference to the fact that the dark era of Alabama's civil rights struggles of the 1960s did not have a direct bearing on tourism until nearly thirty years after they took place. In fact, the state seemed to work hard at making sure those old times there *were* forgotten. But all of that changed in 1988, with the opening of the Birmingham Civil Rights Institute across the street from the civil rights epicenter: the Sixteenth Street Baptist Church.

THE JEFFERSON DAVIS HOME, MONTGOMERY, ALA.

Jefferson Davis's Montgomery home, also known as the "First White House of the Confederacy," was turned into an attraction in 1921. This postcard was mailed in 1912, at which time the building was not yet looking its best.

Inasmuch as that neighborhood also contained such landmarks as Kelly Ingram Park, soon the entire area was being considered a historic district. But Birmingham was not the only location where such history took place. The entire route of 1965's Selma-to-Montgomery march (which did not end well) was also designated a historic trail, with annual re-creations of the famed procession. Suddenly, tourism officials realized that instead of burying such history, it made sense to embrace it.

In some areas, the juxtaposition was rather jarring. Montgomery's tributes to the work of Martin Luther King had to rub shoulders with the First White House of the Confederacy (opened as an attraction in 1921) and the brass star on the steps of the capitol building marking the spot where Jefferson Davis became the first and only Confederate president. Between Clanton and Montgomery, the Sons of Confederate Veterans erected a huge flagpole with a mammoth Confederate flag (naturally, it was the infamous battle flag) next to I-65. But tourists, the ultimate judges of the industry, continue to flock to both genres of attractions, so neither appears to be going away anytime soon.

An interesting sidelight about civil rights tourism: while most attractions are meant to preserve the "good old days," for those who remember them, the Civil Rights Institute, the Selma-to-Montgomery Historic Trail and others are among the only ones to so eagerly present the "bad old days," as well, for the benefit of educating those who were not alive to witness them firsthand. Perhaps the coexistence of both types of attractions can be seen as a fitting metaphor for life itself.

Not-So-Looney Tunes

Say, speaking of the Confederacy, did you hear the one about the county that seceded from Alabama? If you have, you know that the county was Winston, which takes great pride in that historical distinction. It seems that as the Civil War was germinating, and Alabama decided to secede from the Union to join its brers as one of the Confederate States, the people in Winston County didn't think much of the idea. They were not necessarily on the Union's side, either; they simply wanted to be left out of the whole dispute. In the end, that did not work out so well for them—but then, Alabama's secession from the United States didn't turn out that great, either.

For a long time, Winston County held an annual Free State Festival to commemorate its rebellion against the rebels, and in 1987 something new was added. Playwright Lanny McAlister penned a musical he called *The Incident at Looney's Tavern*, based on the meeting at the local watering hole where the decision was made to ditch the rest of the state. It was intended as a one-time-only production in a shopping center parking lot, but somehow the quirky play, sprinkled with songs and what has been termed "hill country humor," grabbed unexpected headlines. For 1988, it was performed in a high school football stadium, and by 1989 construction was underway on a new outdoor amphitheater to serve as the play's permanent home. In 1993, the musical was decreed Alabama's Official Outdoor Musical Drama.

So many people flocked to the amphitheater to see the legend of Looney's Tavern unfold that, naturally, a whole amusement complex grew up around it. More and more features were added over the years, including a 275-seat indoor theater to complement the 1,500-seat amphitheater. An old-fashioned paddle-wheel riverboat, the *Free State Lady*, paddled its wheel around an adjoining branch of Smith Lake, while landlubbers enjoyed a restaurant and gift shop on the shore. There was even a Civil War–themed miniature golf course (Looney Putt) on the premises.

The Story of Alabama Tourism

LOONEY'S Tavern©

"THE AFTERMATH AND THE LEGACY"

Double Springs, Alabama
June 13 – October 12, 1996

Winston County's attempt to secede from the rest of Alabama, rather than take sides in the Civil War, was commemorated in the outdoor musical *The Incident at Looney's Tavern*, performed in its own park at Double Springs throughout the 1990s.

One enduring form of roadside attraction has been the re-created pioneer village. This example could be found near Dauphin Island, but similar-looking brethren existed on U.S. 72 near Athens and U.S. 231 near Troy, among others.

So, if this were such a major attraction alongside U.S. 278, why can't it be visited today? That is an excellent question, and it would be terrific if there were an excellent answer. While the beginning of the Looney's Tavern play and park are well documented, and major articles about it appeared seemingly every year, its eventual demise remains more than a little cloudy. The Alabama Department of Archives and History sums it up in a single sentence: "The program was discontinued in the 2000s and the drama is no longer produced." Newspaper clippings are of little more help. A 2001 tourism directory to outdoor dramas still being produced in America lists *The Incident at Looney's Tavern* as one of two such plays in Alabama—the other, of course, being the apparently immortal *The Miracle Worker* at Ivy Green. The final newspaper article in the Department of Tourism's Looney's Tavern file is from August 2002, and gives no indication that the drama and the park are in any danger of closing. Until more information comes along, we can simply say that at some point during the ensuing ten years, Looney's Tavern Entertainment Park seceded from the list of Alabama tourist attractions. Aerial photos show that the amphitheater and other structures still stand, but a locked gate blocks the former access road, and the attraction today is as obscure as the Free State of Winston.

At about the same time the musical performers were first singing Looney's tunes, another attraction with a historical theme was growing alongside State Highway 69 near Oakman. Old York, USA, begun in 1989, was a collection of a dozen vintage buildings, moved to a single piece of property and restored to something resembling their original appearance. The description sounded faintly like another attempt to get Dry Gulch Ghost Town and Legiontown, USA, done right: "Step 100 years back in time at Old York, a town on the edge of the wild west in the 1800s. Buildings include a saloon, country store, blacksmith shop, log church and cabin." The Bull Pen Steak House was also on the premises. Similar re-created pioneer communities pulled into Troy, alongside U.S. 231, and on U.S. 72 between Athens and Huntsville.

A re-created community of a different sort was Old Alabama Town, actually a district near downtown Montgomery. It had its origins in the early 1970s, when the nonprofit Landmarks Foundation purchased the historic Ordeman House and began restoration work; by the 1980s, Old Alabama Town contained more than forty such structures in a three-block area. Unlike the would-be western towns that more or less resembled the public's collective vision gleaned from movies and television, Old Alabama Town chose the slogan: "See the South the way it really was!"

Renaissance Men

Hey, you know something? Alabama had tried (and sometimes failed, sometimes succeeded) at practically every type of attraction that could be found in any other tourist area—theme parks, goofy miniature golf courses, Wild West towns, museums devoted to either the inspiring or just plain weird—but one tourism staple had slipped by everyone somehow. Just about any area catering to tourists had some sort of observation tower for surveying the surrounding countryside, but about the closest Alabama came to that was Vulcan's observation deck. Panama City Beach had a tower; Hot Springs, Arkansas, had a tower; for a long time, even the top of Stone Mountain near Atlanta had a tower. So where could Alabama put one?

The answer might not have been the most obvious one, but it was in Florence, perched on a bluff overlooking Wilson Dam. The towering tower would be some three hundred feet tall, topped with a restaurant

In 1991, the Renaissance Tower arose on a bluff overlooking the Tennessee River at Florence. The top contained a revolving restaurant with a spectacular view of the surrounding scenery.

as well as an observation deck, and since it would look down at the Tennessee River far below the dam, the total height would be closer to five hundred feet. It was to be the centerpiece of a complex known as the Alabama Information and Exhibit Center, considered a welcome center of sorts for those entering the state through the northwest corner. At the groundbreaking ceremonies, Governor Guy Hunt expressed high hopes:

"Our tourism slogan is 'Alabama, State of Surprises.' But I'll be the one who is surprised if this spot does not become one of the major tourist attractions in the southeastern United States."

Its home had a name, but initially the tower did not. In the early stages, it was being referred to as the "TVA Space Needle," but perhaps realizing Seattle had already laid claim to that moniker, in December 1989 the Tennessee Valley Authority teamed up with Coca-Cola and the Florence Chamber of Commerce to sponsor a "name the tower" contest. The winner would receive a three-day cruise for two to the Bahamas, plus $500 spending money. (No one commented on the irony that even Alabama's tourism moguls would send the winner somewhere else as a prize.)

By February 1990, the winning name had been chosen—Renaissance Tower—and construction was proceeding on schedule. The grand opening was held on May 4, 1991, thus ensuring that tourists in Alabama could have just as much fun looking down on their peers as those in other states. Today, the Renaissance Tower is part of the Marriott Shoals Resort and Spa, and the revolving restaurant at the top is known as the 360 Grille.

At about the same time the tower idea was hatching in Florence, in nearby Muscle Shoals there was another plan to promote tourism. The Alabama Music Hall of Fame released a 45rpm record titled "Alabama Has It All," performed by—sit down for this one—twenty-five state legislators from Morgan, Limestone and Lawrence Counties. The song was penned by Hall of Fame board member James Joiner, who told reporters how he and co-writer Jimmy Durham came up with the theme: "We talked about the different attractions, streams, rivers and mountains around the state and decided those were some of the things we wanted to include in the song." The lyrics ended up mentioning Vulcan, the mountains around Fort Payne and the docks at Mobile, among other sights.

The record was released as a fundraiser to build a $4.5 million Alabama Music Hall of Fame complex near Muscle Shoals. Even its participants knew that those who purchased the record were doing so to support the cause and the state it represented, not to hear their local senator croon a tune. Representative Ernest Dillard of Courtland broke it down to its simplest level: "We were more or less classified into who could sing high and who could sing low. I think the record will be a great advertisement for Alabama."

Peachy Keen

A whole bunch of pages ago, we saw the crippling effect I-65 had on central Alabama's famed peach industry when it first siphoned tourist traffic away from former main road U.S. 31. Over the years, both tourists and farmers grew accustomed to the new way of doing things, and eventually the peach-based stores and restaurants simply migrated out to the exits along the interstate.

By 1993, all of this new business clustered so closely together was making a wreck out of the water pressure in the neighborhood, and the City of Clanton determined that a new water tower was needed. Inspired by a sight he had seen near Gaffney, South Carolina, Clanton mayor Billy Joe Driver decided that as long as a water tower had to be built anyway, it might be a good idea to make it an oddity that could be its own roadside attraction. At a cost of $1.1 million, the tank was fabricated to look like a giant peach, complete with stem, green leaf and cleft. (To put things into perspective, the peach industry was bringing in about $5 million annually to the area.)

Chicago Bridge and Iron was enlisted to do the physical manufacturing of the gargantuan fuzzy fruit, which was delivered to Clanton in pieces to be fitted together like a giant jigsaw puzzle. The peach-shaped water tower was unveiled in October 1993 and is still a landmark at I-65's Exit 212 to this day…along with all the peachy roadside stands it helps advertise.

How to Milk a Motorcycle

For years and years—and then some more years—the Barber family had been famous for their Birmingham-based dairy. Barber's milk and ice cream was a staple of grocery stores and school lunchrooms throughout the state and was somewhat remarkable for the consistency in its packaging. In the mid-1990s, the milk cartons looked pretty much the same as they had in the 1940s. But change was in the formula, and owner George Barber sold the dairy business to concentrate on something he really enjoyed: collecting vintage motorcycles.

Actually, in the 1980s, while still running the dairy, Barber started collecting classic sports cars. He credits David Hooper, manager of the Barber's Dairy delivery fleet, with steering him from cars to motorcycles. In 1995, Barber opened his first Vintage Motorsports Museum in downtown Birmingham, but as anyone who spends much time collecting just about anything will soon learn, it did not take long for the collection to outgrow that original location. By the early 2000s, he had selected a piece of property near I-20 and expanded his museum concept into an entire Barber Motorsports Park.

Proving that the vintage motorcycles in the museum were good for more than sitting in glass cases, the new park featured a 2.38-mile asphalt track on which the display pieces could be taken out and demonstrated. Even the garage where new old acquisitions were repaired and restored was open for the public's inspection. As a phenomenally successful tourist attraction, Barber Vintage Motorsports Park obviously has a powerful appeal to a wide cross-section of the public. But perhaps no one is as proud of the 1,300-strong motorcycle collection as George Barber himself. "They clearly are art to me," he says. "It's like looking at a painting."

Blurry Vision

If you will take just a moment to reflect, you will recall that throughout this book have been examples of how one particular genre of tourist attraction never managed to grab onto its usual success when it came to Alabama, that being the venerable amusement park (and its offspring, the Disney-style theme park). In May 1998, Alabama got its most ambitious attempt to glom onto the ever-more-lucrative theme park market—and it would be one of the most resounding thuds ever heard in the state.

The would-be Walt behind this project was Larry Langford, mayor of Fairfield. In the summer of 1995, he revealed his plans to spend $39 million on a three-hundred-acre theme park near I-59 at Bessemer, and reaction from the public was both supportive and skeptical. Chief among the latter's proponents was the feeling that $39 million could not build much of a park. Among those who felt differently was Birmingham mayor Richard Arrington, who optimistically predicted that someday the venerable Birmingham Zoo might move from its Lane Park home to the new theme park.

A press release from the office of Governor Fob James on April 11, 1996, was probably the first many people had heard of this impending project. On that date, James signed a bill "that will put Alabama on the amusement park map," as the press release put it. Were those words echoing in the distant reaches of Space City, USA? No one could tell, but Langford had certainly done his homework. With promises to take all the business away

No amusement park or theme park had ever been able to make a success of itself in Alabama, and when VisionLand opened near Bessemer in 1998, it kept up the tradition by declaring bankruptcy within a year. After many tortured attempts to stay alive, in 2012 the owners sold off all the amusement rides and converted it into a water park known as Splash Adventure.

from Six Flags Over Georgia and Opryland, he had talked eleven cities into contributing money to form (and be part of) the West Jefferson Amusement and Public Park Authority. Besides Birmingham, the other ten theme park tycoons were Adamsville, Bessemer, Brighton, Fairfield, Hueytown, Lipscomb, Maytown, North Johns, Sylvan Springs and Vance. It should be noted that other than Birmingham and Bessemer, none of them had ever counted tourism among their major industries.

One of Langford's favorite quotations was: "When there is no vision, the people perish." Because Langford insisted that he had a "vision" for revitalizing the western half of Jefferson County—which indeed needed some sort of shot in the arm after the decline of the coal-mining and steelmaking powerhouses—the name of the new park was to be VisionLand. The first press release gave a projected opening date of December 1997, with an expected annual attendance of 800,000.

An elaborate booklet was prepared, outlining all the rides and attractions VisionLand was to contain in its three hundred acres. If the Space City,

USA plans had sounded wildly impractical in the mid-1960s, the changing technology in the theme park industry during the ensuing thirty years inspired ambitions at VisionLand that hardly anyone could have thought were practical. There were to be numerous themed "lands" in the Disney tradition, including one that would bring Vulcan to life in his own "volcanic kingdom." Another would have a dark ride through a *Lord of the Rings*–type land of fairies and gnomes. With no apparent attempt at irony, another section would represent a western town where the marshal and the bad guys would shoot it out—with *water pistols*, daaaaaagnabbit! And those were just a few of them. With stock photography taken from other amusement parks and ride manufacturers' catalogues, the booklet promised a wonderful world of entertainment that would make even Disney dizzy.

The intended December 1997 opening date came and went with no opening. In fact, the opening was set for the very time of year VisionLand would never be open. Instead, the gates swung open in May 1998, but not exactly on the wonderland outlined in the pre-construction publicity. Instead of three hundred acres, the park encompassed seventy, with 10 percent of that being the Steel Waters water park. Most traces of the Disney-styled lands were gone, and the emphasis was on standard rides. Coaster enthusiasts could muster up at least some enthusiasm for "Rampage," billed as Alabama's largest wooden roller coaster (it may, indeed, have been the only one still in operation at the time). There was the 120-foot-tall Sky Wheel, a steel kiddie coaster dubbed "Marvel Mania" and an arcade given the not-so-surprising name "Langford High School," after you-know-who. Admission to all of this would set an adult back twenty-one dollars for a general admission ticket.

What happened next? If VisionLand thought it was going to keep people from traveling to Georgia, Florida and Tennessee for their amusement park fix, it needed its eyes examined. For the 1999 season, two more attractions were added: the Wild River Gorge whitewater ride (Six Flags Over Georgia had had one of those since 1982) and "Dino Domain," which came closest to delivering the type of entertainment promised at the outset. In a wooded area, a trail meandered past animatronic dinosaurs, but this page right out of history became extinct after that single season. The expensive animated monsters were left to decay and dry rot in place. During that season, the park lost $7 million.

The years that followed were not pretty. By February 2000, the famed Cedar Fair amusement company of Sandusky, Ohio, had made arrangements to take over operation of VisionLand from the West Jefferson Amusement Park Authority. The park was hemorrhaging money so fast that the VisionLand name was becoming a liability rather than an asset.

An outlet mall being built near the park announced in September 2000 that it would be known as Watermark Place rather than VisionLand Outlet Center. And the fun just kept on. In 2002, VisionLand filed Chapter 9 bankruptcy and was purchased for $6 million by Southland Entertainment Group. This represented a loss of $59 million in the public funds used to build the bottomless money pit. Southland made a valiant attempt to keep adding new rides—mostly coasters or water-based ones—for the next few years but by 2006 belatedly realized that the Visionland name (they had chosen to drop the enigmatic upper case L in 2003) was poison. The name became Alabama Adventure.

Only then did things get a little brighter, but considering how dark they were before, that wasn't saying much. The "new" Alabama Adventure embarked on an ambitious series of summer concerts, which often brought in stars from such youth-oriented networks as Nickelodeon and the Disney Channel for personal appearances. As happens so often in the theme park business, the park was sold again in 2008, this time to Adrenaline Family Entertainment, headed by a former general manager of Six Flags Over Texas.

Finally, Alabama Adventure threw in the towel—literally. In January 2012, the park received yet another new owner: Amusement Aquatic Management Group. These folks could obviously see what anyone reading this book knows by this point: Alabama folks might enjoy amusement parks, but they would rather go to another state to visit them. What they did want, dating all the way back to the 1960s, were water parks, so Alabama Adventure changed its name to Splash Adventure and sold off every one of the amusement rides except the ones in the water-based area. Since the story of Splash Adventure is still being written, it is anyone's guess what will be the final fate of this tortured entertainment facility.

(Incidentally, when Larry Langford was eventually sent to federal prison on multiple counts of corruption, none of them appeared to stem directly from the VisionLand debacle. However, that did not stop most people from bringing up the park's dismal failure to live up to the promises he had made to those eleven municipalities that got stuck paying for it.)

Discover Yourself

During the same summer that VisionLand was welcoming its first visitors who weren't there, another major attraction in the Birmingham area was getting

The Story of Alabama Tourism

The Red Mountain Museum overlooked the cut through the mountain that formed the new route of U.S. 31. The museum later merged with the nearby Discovery Place to become today's McWane Science Center.

ready to open, but it would have a much happier reception from the general public. This one actually had its origins more than twenty years earlier.

In the late 1960s and early '70s, construction moved at a snail's pace to build the Red Mountain Expressway, an interstate-like thoroughfare that would replace the old twisting route of U.S. 31. The giant cut through Red Mountain exposed millions of years of paleontology all in one place, and the scientific community knew it had a unique opportunity to study the geological history of the area. With that thought in mind, the Red Mountain Museum was chartered by the city in 1971 to document, preserve and display the prehistoric relics unearthed by the highway construction. The museum perched on a bluff overlooking the cut and featured a courtyard with a fiberglass green dinosaur statue that had seen former employment at a Sinclair gas station.

In 1977, another museum opened nearby. Known as Discovery Place, it was a typical "hands-on" facility so popular among the younger crowd where kids could perform their own experiments and learn about how things worked. A big problem faced by both museums was the question of access. Neither was exactly easy to get to and required much involved travel (and sometimes parking) in the mountainous residential areas surrounding them.

In the early 1990s, the two museums merged into one, which was given the name Discovery 2000, and the search was on for a new facility that would be large enough to hold their combined missions. This led them to downtown Birmingham, where the four-story edifice that had formerly housed the iconic Loveman's department store was sitting vacant. Built in 1934–35 after Loveman's original 1890s structure burned to the ground, the once-gleaming Art Deco monolith was beginning to show its age. Loveman's had gone out of business in the spring of 1980, leaving its flagship store to slowly decay from the inside out. Discovery 2000 made a deal with the city to lease the building and set about to reverse more than a dozen years of neglect in preparation for opening it to the public once again.

By the time the new science museum debuted in July 1998, the name had been changed. Actually, everyone knew that "Discovery 2000" was a temporary moniker at best, since it would be obsolete once the calendar rolled over from 2000 to 2001. To the rescue, in more ways than one, came the charitable McWane Foundation, operated by the family of one of Birmingham's earliest steel mill barons. The foundation contributed some $10 million to help finish the project, in gratitude for which Discovery 2000 became the McWane Center in February 1997. (A few years later, the name was further sharpened, and it is now the McWane Science Center.)

The McWane Center was the type of success that VisionLand never even approached being. It utilized all but the very top floor of the huge former store, and while concentrating on its hands-on science exhibits and demonstrations, it took pains to preserve as many as possible of Loveman's original 1935 architectural elements. What was formerly the bargain basement was transformed into an aquarium, with saltwater creatures in one section and another area re-creating a typical Alabama forest stream with native plants and fish. The prehistoric bones and other artifacts dug out of Red Mountain were carefully preserved in another part of the building.

Speaking of that, what of the original Red Mountain Museum building? By the spring of 2007, it had sat abandoned for so long that it was in even worse shape than Loveman's had been. Vegetation was actually growing inside the structure, and in the small park outside, the unemployed Sinclair brontosaurus could no longer even watch the traffic on the expressway because vandals had chopped off his head. Finally, the city agreed to sell the decrepit museum building to St. Rose Academy, a Catholic school, which planned to demolish it for parking. The city retained the park and headless dinosaur, along with the entrance to the Red Mountain cut that had spurred the whole project four decades earlier.

Rust in Piece

Sometimes, in all the excitement of new attractions and their high hopes, the older ones could be a bit neglected—nearly to the dreaded point of no return. That is precisely what happened to an Alabama landmark while all eyes were focused elsewhere.

Since Vulcan Park's much-heralded remodeling in the early 1970s, the facility had pretty much been expected to stay on track and take care of itself. That went for old Ironsides too, who of course was nearly forty years older than the park bearing his name. During the 1980s, preservationists became alarmed at the visibly deteriorating condition of the park and the statue, but no one seemed to be listening. In 1989, Birmingham's WVTM-TV produced a documentary, *Old Man on the Mountain*, to commemorate Vulcan's eighty-fifth anniversary. It illustrated, in gory, graphic detail, just how bad conditions had gotten. In the base of the 1970s pedestal, what had begun as a museum of Vulcan's history had deteriorated into cobweb-infested display cases with much of their explanatory text peeled away by time and neglect. Up in the enclosed observation platform, the relative seclusion had inspired any number of graffiti enthusiasts to splatter the walls with profanity, and that went for the old original stairwell inside the pedestal too.

Even without these difficulties, the Vulcan statue was feeling his age, and showing it too. Many of the problems could be traced back to when the iron man was first anchored to the pedestal in the late 1930s. At that time, great pride was taken in the fact that the hollow giant had been filled to the chest with concrete to stabilize the figure in any sort of weather. Well, weather had managed to get back at Vulcan in other ways. Since iron and concrete react differently to heat and cold, Vulcan's expanding and contracting insides had popped many of the seams and rivets that held him together, and concrete could be seen seeping out of many of those openings. Rust was also an enemy—not surprising when a figure made entirely of iron was involved. For most of his years atop Red Mountain, Vulcan had been painted a shiny, metallic silver color, but during the latter part of the 1970s, his paint job was changed to reddish-brown. Those who asked were told it was to make him the color of real iron ore, but there were strong opinions that it was done merely to camouflage the rust streaks that increasingly pockmarked his iron hide.

In 1991, *Alabama Heritage* magazine quoted iron industry specialists who said the expected lifespan of well-maintained outdoor ornamental iron was about ninety years. Vulcan was approaching his ninetieth anniversary in 1994, and he was nowhere near well maintained. Even the traffic safety torch was a frequent victim of neglect, with only a few of its green (or, at more unfortunate times, red) neon tubes working.

Everything nearly came crashing down in the spring of 1999. An analysis of the park's condition revealed that Vulcan had degenerated from the symbol of a city into a menace to society. There was a real danger that parts of the bare-bottomed behemoth would begin falling off and possibly landing on visitors below. (One wonders whether the torch would have been changed to red on such an occasion.) Finally, there was nothing left to do but close the park until solutions could be studied and money raised to implement them. By May, the gates were closed and padlocked, and it looked like one of the state's oldest and most famous attractions was headed for the scrap heap.

Chapter 6
Heading Toward the Horizon

It should go without saying that the closer one gets to the present day, the more difficult it becomes to recognize what is truly historic and what only seems so. It takes the passage of time to be able to look back at things and see them clearly. Sorry, folks, that's just the way it was set up several millennia ago. So, it is not that nothing has happened in Alabama tourism since the 1990s gave way to the 2000s, but it is too soon to tell what will have any permanent effect on this long-established enterprise. With that thought in mind, we will briefly wrap up this whole discussion with a look at how the twenty-first century has treated some of the old-time attractions that have been introduced in the previous pages.

Horse Pens 40, Alabama's answer to Rock City, had closed in 1994 after the death of its owner, Warren Musgrove. The property sat there for six years—fortunately, the rock formations had already survived a few million years, so a few more did not change them—until coming under new ownership and reopening around 2000. Today, it operates much as it always did, enticing travelers off of U.S. 231 and to the top of the mountain for scenic views, handicrafts and all the rest.

An even older attraction threatened to erase its name from Alabama road maps in September 2002, when Jasmine Hill Gardens at Wetumpka announced that it would close after seventy years. Owners Jim and Elmore Inscoe told reporters that they were looking at some new uses for the gardens, but at least in this case, the death sentence did not seem to be a permanent one. Jasmine Hill Gardens is now open again, albeit on a more limited time schedule than in the old days, and the Fitzpatricks' priceless collection of Greek art and artifacts can still be enjoyed by those who care to look it up.

One of the greatest success stories of the 2000s involved Vulcan Park. We have already seen that at the end of the 1990s, the park had been padlocked because of the deteriorating condition of the giant iron statue, and the rest of the grounds were going to seed as well. The public responded overwhelmingly to Vulcan's plight, and $14 million was raised to get things up and running again. Unlike the early 1970s facelift Vulcan Park had received, the goal this time was not renovation but restoration.

Everything was geared toward putting the park back to resembling its original late 1930s look. Fortunately, when the ugly marble sheathing was removed, it was found that the original WPA-era stonework of the original pedestal was still mostly intact, and repairing the damage would not be as difficult as feared. The public still needed an alternative to climbing all those stairs, though, so a lot of thought was put into how to make an elevator blend in with the new old look. The narrow shaft was finally placed in such a way that when viewed from most angles, it would be hidden by the larger pedestal. The enclosed observation deck reverted to the original-style open-air metal platform, from which visitors could easily view Vulcan's prodigious posterior looming over them.

One original element that could not be replicated was the series of cascading pools and their goldfish. However, the area where they used to be was landscaped in a series of descending terraces that mimicked the pools' original shape. (And of course, there was always the option of rebuilding the pools at some future date.) A new museum building was constructed, using twenty-first-century technology to give Vulcan's story from the World's Fair to the present, paralleling the ups and downs his hometown had experienced.

And speaking of those problems, what about Vulcan himself? The ultimate solution was to take him apart, repair and restore him piece by piece and then reassemble him atop the pedestal. For almost four years, residents and tourists looked up at Red Mountain to see only an empty pedestal while the big guy got ready to face his second century. This time, instead of the troublesome concrete filling, Vulcan was fitted around a metal skeleton that would serve the purposes of stabilization without affecting the well-being of his iron skin.

One controversial decision was to not retain the 1946 traffic safety torch. If the goal was to re-create Vulcan Park as it originally was, the torch had to go. Once again, Vulcan held up his spear point toward the heavens, and the torch—which, after all, many people considered a historic artifact

After a massive renovation project, Vulcan Park reopened in 2004 with the statue, pedestal and grounds restored to their original 1939 appearance.

anyway—was installed in the new museum, where the push of a button would light up its green neon tubes to remind everyone of how it used to function. The new Vulcan Park opened in March 2004, just in time for a celebration of Vulcan's centennial.

Another restoration project, on a hunk of iron that was even larger than Vulcan, involved the USS *Alabama*. Since it arrived in Mobile in 1964, the *Alabama* had been sitting in twenty feet of mud, and nearly forty years of that had left the battleship battle scarred. In June 2002, the water level around the ship was lowered so inspectors could get a close-up view of the part of the hull that normally sat below the waterline. What they found was not pretty: the bottom of the ship was badly corroded and needed to be double-plated to ensure its survival. The new war cry of Battleship Memorial Park became: "She protected our freedom; help preserve her future!"

Another round of restoration took place a decade later. An anniversary celebration was planned for August 2012, commemorating seventy years since the *Alabama* was commissioned. Battleship Memorial Park was still a major factor in Mobile's share of the tourism pie, and fundraising commenced to help renovate the facility. Just as with the Vulcan project, the ultimate goal was to put the USS *Alabama* back to as close to its original appearance as possible. In addition, a new audio tour would feature the reminiscences of some of the surviving crew members who had served on the battleship during World War II.

In the late summer of 2005, Hurricane Katrina pounded the Gulf Coast once again, but unlike Hurricane Frederic's unwelcome visit in 1979, this time most of the damage took place west of Alabama, where Biloxi and Gulfport, Mississippi, were nearly erased from the landscape. As was the case after Frederic, Mobile's Bellingrath Gardens suffered the most of any veteran Alabama attraction. However, while the gardens were closed for six months to recover from Frederic, after Katrina it took only two and a half weeks to get them back into shape—and that was primarily because of the loss of electricity. The storm surge was estimated at ten feet, but since the gardens and Bellingrath home were twenty feet above the river, damage was once again confined mainly to the loss of some trees.

No matter what natural events affected the tourism industry, there was always the need to promote it, letting those both inside and out of the state know just what awaited them. In the spring of 2012, Birmingham advertising firm Luckie & Co. embarked on the latest in a long line of tourism promotions, this time designed around the theme of a classic 1953 Cadillac stopping off at highlighted attractions including the Birmingham Zoo, the Space and Rocket Center and Barber Motorsports Park. Sounding like an echo from the long-ago post–World War II days, Luckie & Co. creative officer Brad White told the press, "Alabama's been a drive-through state. We're trying to make it a drive-to state." Yes, things never really change—only the names and details are different.

Since there is no valid way to end this story that has no ending, perhaps it is best to wrap things up here with an attraction that relates back to one of the early discussions in the first chapter of this book. Senator William Bankhead,

The Story of Alabama Tourism

The former home of William Bankhead (namesake of the Bankhead National Forest and the father of Tallulah) in Jasper has now been opened as a history museum. It stands not far from the former Bankhead Highway, named in honor of William's father, John Hollis Bankhead.

the son of Senator John Hollis Bankhead and father of stage and screen legend Tallulah Bankhead, built an impressive home in Jasper, only a few blocks from the Bankhead Highway that was named in honor of his father's pioneering "good roads" efforts. The house saw a lot of history over the years, including Tallulah's wedding in 1937, and when William Bankhead died in 1940, Washington dignitaries overran the property to pay their respects at the funeral. (President Roosevelt was the most prominent of those.)

Seventy years later, the old Bankhead home became an attraction itself: a museum of local Walker County history, just as the Bankhead family had been responsible for the creation of a good portion of Alabama's early tourism. Still near the former Bankhead Highway and just down the road from the Bankhead National Forest, the public opening of the Bankhead House and Heritage Center proved that, indeed, the story of the Alabama tourism industry was not ending in the moldy past—only continuing toward the sunrise on the distant horizon of the future.

Bibliography

Books

Bellingrath Gardens and the Bellingrath Home. Mobile, AL: Bellingrath-Morse Foundation, 1958.
Crownover, Danny Kenneth. *Black Creek: Southern Lookout Mountain*. Gadsden, AL: self-published, 1983.
Dora Centennial: Scrapbook of Memories. Dora, AL: Davis Printing, 1986.
Drinnon, Elizabeth McCants. *Stuckey: The Biography of Williamson Sylvester Stuckey*. Macon, GA: Mercer University Press, 1997.
Faris, John T. *Seeing the Sunny South*. Philadelphia: J.B. Lippincott Co., 1921.
Hall, Lynne L. *Strange But True Alabama*. Alabaster, AL: Sweet Water Press, 2005.
Hollis, Tim. *Dixie Before Disney: 100 Years of Roadside Fun*. Jackson: University Press of Mississippi, 1999.
———. *Loveman's: Meet Me Under the Clock*. Charleston, SC: The History Press, 2012.
———. *See Rock City: The History of Rock City Gardens*. Charleston, SC: The History Press, 2009.
Jackson, Harvey H., III. *The Rise and Decline of the Redneck Riviera: An Insider's History of the Florida-Alabama Coast*. Athens: University of Georgia Press, 2012.

Norton, Bertha Bendall. *Birmingham's First Magic Century*. Birmingham, AL: Lakeshore Press, 1970.

Preston, Howard Lawrence. *Dirt Roads to Dixie: Accessibility and Modernization in the South, 1885–1935*. Knoxville: University of Tennessee Press, 1991.

Rowell, Raymond, Sr. *Vulcan in Birmingham*. Birmingham, AL: Birmingham Park and Recreation Board, 1972.

Satterfield, Carolyn Green. *The Birmingham Botanical Society: A Brief History*. Birmingham, AL: Birmingham Botanical Society, 1999.

Sermons in Stone: The Life and Work of Brother Joseph. Chicago: Curt Teich & Co., 1965.

This Is Alabama. Montgomery, AL: State Division of Records and Reports, 1946.

NEWSPAPER AND MAGAZINE ARTICLES

Aiken, Boone. "New Welcome Center Busy Spot." *Birmingham News*, August 16, 1977.

———. "Progress Is Proving Fatal as Highways Skirt Towns." *Birmingham News*, June 18, 1961.

Alabama Living. "Fit for a King." January 1981.

Associated Press. "Jasmine Hill Gardens, Museum Will Close." September 9, 2002.

Ausbun, Danny. "Iron-Steel Museum Will Be Fitting New Attraction at Tannehill Park." *Birmingham News*, August 6, 1980.

Beckwith, Alisa. "Small-Town Pride in Natural Bridge." *Tuscaloosa News*, February 10, 2002.

Beiman, Irving. "Huge Smith Dam will be dedicated next Tuesday." *Birmingham News*, May 21, 1961.

Bigbee, Nelle. "Ivy Green Reopens Saturday." *Birmingham News*, October 20, 1972.

Birmingham News. "Boundary Lines Approved for Horseshoe Bend Park." June 17, 1957.

———. "Don't Cover Disputed State Motto at Tourist Center, Orders Wallace." May 16, 1977.

———. "Folsom Opens Gulf Highway on the Fourth." June 16, 1949.

———. "Fort Payne's Manitou Cave Is Nearby Scenic Wonder. " June 17, 1962.

Bibliography

———. "Green Light Given to Start Renovation at Vulcan Park." November 27, 1969.
———. "Harpersville Speed Trap Broken Up." February 17, 1952.
———. "New Highway Between Here, Capital to Open." November 24, 1960.
———. "Noccalula Statue Will Be Unveiled in Gadsden Sunday." September 19, 1969.
———. "Park Centered on Water Sports Opens Saturday." May 19, 1972.
———. "People are Behind Speed Curb." November 16, 1953.
———. "Purchase of Landmark for Shrine Urged." June 16, 1952.
———. "State Fair Authority Pushes Park Plan." May 22, 1969.
———. "Work Begun on Bessemer Road." January 1, 1936.
Bleiberg, Larry. "Barber's Bikes." *Alabama Journey* (September–October 2011).
Bolton, Mike. "All That's Left of the Bottle Is the Name." *Birmingham News*, undated clipping.
Bunch, Joey. "Canyonland Dream Unfulfilled but Still Alive." *Fort Payne Times-Journal*, February 27, 1988.
Burnett, Emmett. "Blindsided!" *Alabama Living*, September 2009.
Cason, Mike. "Ex-Horse Pens Owner Warren Musgrove Dies." *Birmingham News*, May 11, 2005.
Chattanooga Times. "Borden Is Named to Cavrens Post." April 12, 1969.
———. "KOA Will Build at Valley Head." April 26, 1970.
———. "Rock City Will Operate and Develop Sequoyah Caverns." March 30, 1969.
Cherokee County Herald. "Battleship Is Open Again." October 10, 1979.
Coman, Victoria. "Vote on Selling Museum Site to St. Cecilia Nuns Expected." *Birmingham News*, May 15, 2007.
Coosa Valley Co-Op Edition. "DeSoto Caverns; Home of KyMulga Onyx Cave." March 1976.
Daily Mountain Eagle. "Things to See and Do in Walker County." September 26, 1997.
Dollar, June. "Legislators Sing in Favor of Alabama's Hall of Fame." *Decatur Daily*, August 16, 1987.
Dothan Eagle. "Wave Pool, Water Slide Opening May 3." April 30, 1980.
East Lauderdale News. "Name the Tower Contest." December 14, 1989.
———. "Renaissance Tower Going Up in Florence." February 8, 1990.
Finch, Jackie. "Even Katrina Can't Stop This City's Mum Festival." *Hoosier Times*, November 13, 2005.

Bibliography

Fort Payne Times-Journal. "Newest Shrine Added to Ave Maria Grotto." March 4, 1995.

Fox, Al. "Scrap Heap or Memorial: Which for Proud Lady?" *Birmingham News*, July 1962.

Franklin, Rebecca. "'Miracle Worker' Hit on Broadway." *Birmingham News*, October 25, 1959.

Fullman, Lynn Grisard. "McWane Center Promises Science for All Ages." *Huntsville Times*, May 17, 1998.

Gadsden Times. "Little River Canyon Rides Open Tomorrow." March 7, 1970.

Gordon, Tom. "For USS Alabama, It's Action Again." *Birmingham News*, June 6, 1987.

Gray, John. "Tannehill State Park Opens at Iron Industry Birthplace." *Birmingham News*, June 7, 1971.

Harmon, Rick. "Looney Idea." *Montgomery Advertiser*, August 1, 2002.

Hill, Emily. "USS *Alabama*'s 70th Birthday Celebration." *Mobile Press-Register*, August 14, 2012.

Hill, Thomas F. "Ivy Green Burns." *Birmingham News*, April 16, 1972.

House, Jack. "Completion of Highway 241 Gives Eufaula Front, Back Door." *Birmingham News*, December 4, 1941.

———. "Long Dream at Last Realized." *Birmingham News*, December 7, 1941.

Huntsville Times. "New Management Will Run VisionLand." February 11, 2000.

———. "Space City Projects Big Amusement Park." January 19, 1964.

Kemp, Kathy. "Miss Vulcan 1939." *Birmingham News*, September 6, 2007.

Kennedy, James H. "All Regard Clanton's Water Tank as Peachy." *Birmingham News*, October 31, 1993.

Kiplinger, W.M. "Your New $27 Billion Road Map." *This Week*, May 20, 1956.

Kitay, William. "Rolling Gold Flows around Alabama." *Birmingham News*, October 20, 1947.

Loeb, Francis. "How One Motel Franchise System Works." *Tourist Court Journal*, February 1956.

Lowry, Walton. "Gardendale Judge Denies Speed Trap Charges." *Birmingham News*, August 16, 1967.

Malone, Becky. "KyMulga Cave Could Become Major Tourist Attraction." *Talladega Daily Home*, August 14, 1969.

Osborn, Clement. "Alabama's Canyon Booming Tourist Attraction." *DeKalb News*, July 4, 1971.

Rankin, Allen. "A Man, A Cave and A Dream." *Reader's Digest*, June 1962.

Rawls, Phillip. "James Orders Two Confederate Flags to Fly." Associated Press, March 5, 1996.

Richardson, Anwar. "Vision Park's Merry-Go-Round." *Birmingham Post-Herald*, July 28, 1995.

Richardson, Sandee. "Teachers Visit Historic Sites." *Montgomery Advertiser*, July 30, 1998.

Shirley, Robert L. "'Bama History in Log Cabins." *Northwest Alabamian*, May 12, 1963.

Simms, Jimmy. "Looney's Tavern: The Legacy." *Cullman Times*, June 10, 1998.

Simpson, Ami. "Enterprise, Home of the Bug Lady." *Alabama Advocate*, May 12, 1988.

Smithey, Waylon. "Park Modernizing Scars Cheaha." *Birmingham News*, November 20, 1972.

Southern Living. "Ships of State." June 1968.

Sparrow, Hugh W. "Alabama to Start New Highway System." *Birmingham News*, September 16, 1956.

———. "Alabama's Trunk Highways Slated for Streamlining." *Birmingham News*, January 20, 1952.

———. "Big Interchange to Be Started Soon." *Birmingham News*, October 16, 1966.

———. "Superhighway Pattern Shapes Up." *Birmingham News*, March 20, 1960.

———. "U.S. 78 Stretch to Be Four-Laned." *Birmingham News*, July 18, 1957.

Spotswood, James. "100 Years to Get Our Freeways?" *Birmingham News*, October 16, 1962.

Steele, Cameron. "Candy Queen Cora Saxon Dies at 102." *Anniston Star*, June 30, 2010.

Storey, Debroah. "Space City, Amusement Park Proposed in 1960s, Was Never Completed." *Huntsville Times*, March 18, 2012.

Swant, Martin. "A Locally Driven Tourism Plan." *Birmingham News*, April 19, 2012.

Thompson, George Clinton. "Vulcan: Birmingham's Man of Iron." *Alabama Heritage*, Spring 1991.

Tomberlin, Michael. "Forging Ahead." *Birmingham News*, February 16, 2004.

———. "New Splash Adventure to Expand Water Park." *Birmingham News*, April 5, 2012.

Watkins, Ed. "Gas Price Boosts Attendance at Tannehill." *Tuscaloosa News*, July 13, 1980.

Bibliography

———. "Outlook for Tannehill Appears Brighter Now." *Tuscaloosa News*, August 9, 1970.

Whitmire, Kyle. "Park to Lose Up to $7 Million This Year." *Bessemer Western Star*, August 18, 1999.

Websites

www.alabama.travel
www.alabamaminingmuseum.com
www.alapark.com
www.americanroads.us
www.archives.alabama.gov
www.avemariagrotto.com
www.barbermotorsports.com
www.bbgardens.org
www.bcri.org
www.bellingrath.org
www.birminghamrewound.com
www.birminghamzoo.com
www.campjellystone.com
www.dauphinisland.org
www.desotocavernspark.com
www.discoverlookoutmountain.com
www.dismalscanyon.com
www.encyclopediaofalabama.org
www.firstwhitehouse.org
www.fortmorgan.org
www.gulfshores.com
www.helenkellerbirthplace.org
www.historicmobile.com
www.hp40.com
www.hurricanecreek.homestead.com
www.jasminehill.org
www.mcwane.org
www.moundville.ua.edu

www.naturalbridgeal.com
www.nickshell.com
www.pointmallardpark.com
www.roadsideamerica.com
www.rocketcenter.com
www.sequoyahcaverns.com
www.showcaves.com
www.slossfurnaces.com
www.splashadventurewaterpark.com
www.stuckeys.com
www.talladegasuperspeedway.com
www.ussalabama.com
www.visitvulcan.com
www.wacf.org
www.waterworlddothan.com

About the Author

Tim Hollis has been a pop culture historian literally all his life. He likes to tell how, when he was nine years old, he was writing letters and trying to preserve the memories of things from when he was three. This mania for living in the past has resulted in twenty-two books (as of right now, anyway), ranging in subjects from southern tourism nostalgia to Birmingham history to children's television and children's records, among other topics. He also owns a museum of toys, advertising, holiday memorabilia and other baby boomer relics that he makes available to visitors and researchers by appointment. Having lived in Birmingham his entire life, he supplies the nostalgic materials for the popular www.BirminghamRewound.com website, through which he may also be contacted.

Visit us at
www.historypress.net

This title is also available as an e-book